MOURA QUAYLE

DESIGNED LEADERSHIP

Columbia University Press
Publishers Since 1893
New York Chichester, West Sussex
cup.columbia.edu
Copyright © 2017 Columbia University Press
All rights reserved

Library of Congress Cataloging-in-Publication Data
Names: Quayle, Moura, 1951– author.
Title: Designed leadership / Moura Quayle.
Description: New York : Columbia University Press, [2017] |
Includes bibliographical references and index.
Identifiers: LCCN 2016050680 (print) | LCCN 2017011172 (e-book) |
ISBN 9780231173124 (cloth : alk. paper) | ISBN 9780231544689 (e-book)
Subjects: LCSH: Leadership.
Classification: LCC HD57.7 .Q39 2017 (print) | LCC HD57.7 (e-book) |
DDC 658.4/092—dc23
LC record available at https://lccn.loc.gov/2016050680

Columbia University Press books are printed on permanent
and durable acid-free paper.
Printed in the United States of America

ILLUSTRATIONS: Moura Quayle

Contents

Contents

Acknowledgments

There are many people who have helped me with this book: colleagues from the university, business, and government; students from design and business; and, of course, friends and family. To those very special colleagues who read early drafts of the proposal and gave feedback—you know who you are—a big thanks to you for contributing to early momentum.

One university, The University of British Columbia, through talented Presidents and senior administrators, has assisted me in my growth as an academic and a pracademic. For this, I am eternally grateful.

Three Deans helped by providing support and encouragement: Daniel Muzyka of UBC Sauder School of Business, Robert Helsley of UBC Sauder School of Business, and Gage Averill of UBC Faculty of Arts, where the Liu Institute for Global Issues finds its home.

One extraordinary writing mentor and editor, Richard Littlemore, helped by providing interim deadlines and great advice and, in a sense, saving me from myself.

One amazing medieval historian and endnote aficionado, Peter Jones, made sure that citations are correct and more information is available to those who want it.

Two parents, now gone, always encouraged me to be Moura.

And finally thanks to one husband, David Fushtey, whose love and support I feel daily, and whose scholarly talents and editing capacity I cherish.

Designed Leadership

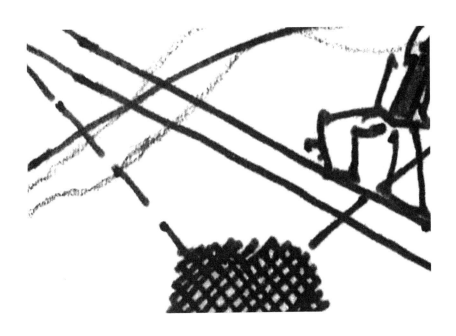

Introduction

Strategic Design in Action

THIS BOOK IS ABOUT HOW to use the mindset, tools, techniques, and methods of design and designers to shape the practice of leadership.

Let's begin by acknowledging that there are plenty of excellent theories about effective leadership. The (virtual) bookstores and back issues of *Fortune* and *Harvard Business Review* are filled with worthy contemplations of leadership styles, with scholarly treatments of well-crafted success. Many of these accounts deserve your attention.

de·sign /də'zīn/ verb: an active approach or process forging toward a result with both utility and elegance.

It is also true that every good leader works "by design"—with a plan and a sense of purpose. But this book is reaching for something more. *Designed Leadership* mines the practices and traditions of the design disciplines to identify a set of tools, techniques, and methods that have proved to be instrumental in creating things that work—objects or processes that do what they were *designed* to do efficiently, reliably, and consistently. In general, these practices are trained or encouraged, as a matter of course, in design schools or in the studios and apprenticeships of the design world; and here we may also grasp some important lessons about where and how we can learn to be better leaders. Anyone trained in design—of whatever kind—eventually finds that the designer's discipline becomes a mindset. And just as good leaders work "by design," some of us happen upon helpful habits of mind without design training or intentional learning. The pages that follow explain why the dividends of designed leadership should not be left to chance. Designers have developed their methodology over many centuries, with care and attention and through trial and error. We can all learn from their mistakes, and in turn practice designed leadership.

January 9, 2016: the spent core of the Falcon 9 rocket explodes on an autonomous drone ship in the Atlantic Ocean. They called it "a hard landing," but given that the 157-foot SpaceX rocket engine was setting down on a violently bobbing robotic barge, the touchdown was surprisingly gentle. The rocket slows, almost to a stop, and then seems to lean, almost in slow motion, as one of its four legs buckles.[1] SpaceX founder Elon Musk called what happened next a "rapid, unscheduled disassembly"—the rocket toppled and blew itself to bits. And with that, "RUD" proliferates as yet another acronym on Twitter.[2]

If you asked a designer to describe the foregoing in a word, she might suggest prototyping or testing or experimenting. Few worthy goals are achieved on the first attempt and without some conscious experimentation. In the context of the SpaceX program to develop

a reusable rocket, this was an iteration, not an endpoint. On March 4,
six weeks after the January "failure," the SpaceX crew slammed
another Falcon 9 lander onto
a barge with a degree of vio-
lence that again destroyed the
rocket—and knocked out the
YouTube feed. Musk shrugged on
Twitter: "Didn't expect this one to work
(v hot re-entry), but next flight has a good
chance." An excellent chance, apparently: on April 8, the next
rocket set down perfectly.[3]

This example is not an argument that Elon Musk is necessarily a practitioner or exemplar of designed leadership. By his own
description, Musk is a "nano-manager," demanding, overbearing,
interfering, and infamously impatient.[4] This is, however, an example of the rigor and the organizational approach that you must
bring to any thoughtful design process.

The value of the strategic design method is its ability to uncover the invisible
or what isn't being revealed and design a path forward; combining the *art* of
discovery, the *science* of generalizability, and the *business* of management
and measurement, suggests Angèle Beausoleil in discussion about her
PhD dissertation on designing the innovation process as a learning model
using strategic design.[5] Angèle defines the strategic design method as
"an approach that involves strategic thinking and reflective action through
the use of creative and critical thinking techniques, resulting in situated
innovation."[6]

The acts of discovery and questioning, the potential for some generaliz-
able solutions and the metrics of business management combine to create a
powerful approach. The strategic design method can be used for every scale
of problem or opportunity. It utilizes design research, design thinking and
design delivery as modes of working. Strategic design drives our thinking
toward transformation, to action and change, to designing something better.

Such an approach can be broken out in the stages of the strategic design method, which is a collaborative, visual, disciplined thinking method for tackling complex problems (small and large) and systemic challenges. It usually involves multidisciplinary teams that blend creative and critical thinking techniques with data analysis to cocreate, test, and develop solutions. It happens in steps.

You first:

ASK, which includes researching, discovering, defining the problem, and scoping. You find facts, you find meaning, and you find opportunities. You precisely clarify the goal you want to achieve, and then you . . .

TRY, which is where Musk and company crashed and burned, again and again, without damaging their program or their reputation. TRY, in this context, includes generating, testing, choosing, and prototyping. You generate ideas and test their effectiveness against your intentions. You choose mandatory and desirable criteria, and then you reflect to discover, for example, why exactly "the lockout collet doesn't latch on one of the four legs." And reflection, in this context, may mean sitting in quiet reverie or picking through the rubble. Finally, you . . .

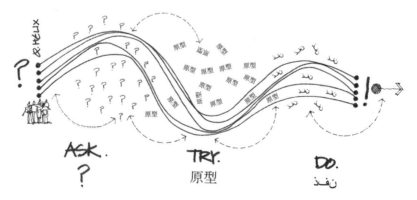

Do. You implement and evaluate, again and again. At this stage, a good designer knows both when to start and never to stop. Even the best products or processes can be improved. You implement, monitor, learn—and repeat.

Of course, not everyone is trying to land a rocket in the Atlantic, buy a ticket to leave the planet, or revolutionize the automobile industry. But the opportunity to design (or to blunder by failing to do so) stands before us at almost every moment of the day. We design each morning when we put on our clothes. We ask ourselves: What am I doing today? What is the weather like? What look do I want? What clothes are clean? We generally ask and answer unconsciously—and we manage to get dressed without fuss. We can, of course, get dressed without design—we all know people who obviously do—but most people take it as a first opportunity to start the day on the right foot.

Designers of various types use design methods as a matter of practice and necessity and, presumably, they may not think much about the practice while immersed in it. But as a built-environment designer (a landscape architect) who has strayed into the fields of education (as a university dean), government (as a senior public servant), policy, organizational transformation, and, inevitably, business, I have found myself digging into my own design tool kit every day. I have sometimes watched in admiration, as leaders around me acted on these principles, by instinct or by design—or in disappointment, as they missed great opportunities by not applying these principles and practices.

Why is designed leadership—the idea of applying design principles and practices to leadership—important now and in the future?

A characteristic of the strategic design method is how we understand,

> Designed leadership uses the mindset, tools, techniques, and methods of design and designers to shape the practice of leadership.

unpack, get into, and explore the problem. Positive people, like advocates of appreciative inquiry (a change-management approach that begins with what is going well, not with what is going wrong) prefer to start with opportunities, not problems.[7] In a world where everything matters, we must identify both the rewards and the risks. Henry Kaiser's approach is a good one.

"Problems are just opportunities in work clothes."

HENRY J. KAISER, CEO KAISER INDUSTRIES, 1949

This book is about developing a shared language and interaction between design and business that will shape more effective leadership. Designed leadership.

Still, we must look at all sides, even when it is difficult to flip back and forth between problems and opportunities. And we must keep asking the questions: What is the problem we want to solve? What are the opportunities that we don't yet see?

Or, put another way, before moving to a discussion about designed leadership as a solution, it's important to be clear about the problems we're trying to solve—and the opportunities we may be missing. That, in itself, is a challenge: in an increasingly complicated world, even the problems are opaque. Through my experience in teaching, in business, in civil society, and in government, I have seen people tripped up by these barriers in their work and in their lives—barriers they frequently built themselves. Here is one way to explain and acknowledge a particular set, or landscape, of challenges that anyone working on complex problems faces daily: we are lost or wandering; we are afraid; and we are illiterate.

We Are Lost—So We Must Find Direction

This observation applies across sectors: in politics, in business, and specifically in the C-suite of the CEO, CFO, COO, CTO, and all the new chiefs. It's a reflection of the complex and new systems that we encounter daily. If we do not have the capacity to identify, question, assess, and move on quickly, it can all become overwhelming, inviting us to wander aimlessly.

We lose our way when we are playing too many roles on too many stages. We all wear many hats: directors, executives, parents, friends, coaches, computer users, financial planners, operations managers, weekend athletes. We stitch these roles together with others in the same boat, trying to stay connected via Twitter, text, or Facebook. Few of us find a community of interests just down the street.

The fragmentation that sets us wandering has its roots in the atomization of information, and in a countervailing oversimplification and abstraction. To these forces we add information technology, which allows us to disengage from the face-to-face and embrace objectification and avatars.

We also get lost because of the desire to simplify things that aren't simple. Often, we have a tough time seeing because we have been taught to expect simple answers—from science or from "experts." And it's partly true: the techno-rational model and way of thinking have produced some pretty amazing ideas and applications. It promotes a sense that science and technology together can tackle any problem, inviting us to sit back and wait for solutions that will provide us with the stable systems we expect and need. But it isn't that simple: resources are not infinite, and it's usually

Physicist Ursula Franklin gets to the heart of the problem with technology.[8] She writes eloquently about the culture of compliance that technology has created—the channel changer doesn't allow us to alight long enough to really see. She is also clear about the separation that technology has wrought since the industrial revolution, when we were more directly involved in every aspect and challenge of day-to-day living—identifying needs, and then identifying solutions or designing and using new tools. Technology has removed us from the whole. We now usually participate in one small piece of the process, and it is hard to get a feel for the whole and take any interest in or ownership of it.[9]

impossible to be fully informed about any of the decisions that we have to make. We are surprised when our models create unexpected and unhappy results. On top of objectification and oversimplification, we also get stuck in abstractions—abstract language, abstract ideas, abstract solutions. We forget to enjoy the journey.

Recognizing that we are lost doesn't mean that we will stop wandering; "Not all who wander are lost."[10] Strategic design is applied wandering, within a framework of milestones and decision points, to ground ourselves in a connected and integrated way to each other and to our challenges. In that context, designed leadership is about wandering with an open mind, a sense of purpose, and courage.

We Are Afraid—So We Must Learn to Take Risks

Nothing stymies creativity like fear. Senior managers must focus on performance, and risk aversion is hardwired into our reptilian brains.[11] When we want to think long-term, with diverse interests in complex ecologies of ideas, these executive functions are forever bumping up against old, nerve-jangling survival instincts and, without training, they are overruled in what cognitive studies refer to as *opposing domains*.[12] We are born curious and open to experimenting; it's what has enabled humans to survive. But modern educational institutions now intervene, often rewarding complacency and compliance rather than fostering an eagerness to ask questions and to test and understand the edges of risk. We tell each other that we honor creativity and we crave innovation, but we are constantly measured by, and rewarded for, our ability to color within the lines.

"There is only one thing that makes a dream impossible to achieve: the fear of failure."

PAULO COELHO, *THE ALCHEMIST*, 1993

We all have fears—fear of heights, fear of people, even fear of success. In leadership, we may fear taking the helm, because we don't know what will happen. This is connected to fear of change, because despite how quickly we know our context is changing and will change, it is hard to face what may come next. These are fears that no one escapes.

Politicians demand measurable standards and are allergic to risk. Professionals learn to assess risk and make informed decisions. Entrepreneurs learn to make decisions based on the information available, favoring an opportunity model of reward.  Yet, we have few prizes—and no degrees—for those who try something wonderful and fail, not even for those who weighed the risks carefully but were tripped up by circumstances they could not antici- pate. So rather than lead, we too often manage in fear. Our challenge is knowing when to listen to our "creative voice," and when to invite our "critical voice" in. We need both of these voices to help us set up frameworks to make good ideas better. We need to recognize and accept that the odd "rapid, unscheduled disassembly" is a necessary part of progress.

We Are Illiterate—So We Must Learn to Communicate

This, of course, is not meant literally. If we have come this far together, we are all—by the dictionary definition—literate to some degree. But literacy also implies a shared and accurate understand- ing, and here, today, we fall short.

To go fast, go alone. To go far, go with others. This has been said a thousand times, in a thousand ways and by people in a hun- dred cultures. More than ever, we must learn how to work and play well with others, and that starts with the words we use to get along. Our global village is compressed in the digital age, and we are acutely aware of all the different cultural and professional languages. "Eighty-five percent of the world's population do not speak English; there are hundreds of belief systems, thousands of languages, and billions of separate educational and experiential perspectives."[13] How can we read others' stories and write stories of our own? How can we share ideas and work together effectively?

Many of our shared frustrations are systemic. They include deficits of personal capacity, like resistance to change or lack of capacity to talk about shared values; or deficits of power or influence, like lack of control over climate change, poverty, social injustice, or the frailties of democracy, marketplace production systems, and consumerism and settlement patterns.[14] Managing systemic change requires a capacity to ask good questions and communicate with each other—in languages that we all can understand.

> "To the uneducated a letter A is just three sticks."
>
> JOAN POWERS, *POOH'S LITTLE INSTRUCTION BOOK*, 1995, INSPIRED BY A. A. MILNE

Yet common understanding is often not even a goal. We love our tribal languages. People pay lip service to integration and crossing disciplines, but in many disciplines, the more exclusive the language, the better. But the more adept we are at being understood within our cliques, the more incapable we may become of communicating beyond their boundaries. The problem lies in translation. Think about how a simple choice of words or an emoji can accelerate communication or stop it dead.

> "Visual culture is not limited to the study of images or media, but extends to everyday practices of seeing and showing."
>
> W. J. T. MITCHELL, IN *JOURNAL OF VISUAL CULTURE*, 2002

The new breed of digital natives needs to be adept both within their clique and across many boundaries. Just as there is a requirement to work with the languages of business (accounting, economics, finance, human resources, law, marketing, and organizational behavior), there is a pressing opportunity to connect these disciplines—their concepts and content—to the interdisciplinary or transdisciplinary lexicon of the design world. This is a challenge because the language of design can also be obscure and confusing. For example, design attaches very specific definitions to words like process, concept, line, shape, edges, boundaries, connections, and context. Even a simple term like "value" can mean something different to a designer than to a stock analyst; value in design can refer to both the integrity and intensity of color, and to the normative quality assigned to any other element or activity.

The language of business and the language of design can translate and inform effective leadership. Designed leadership, the application of design principles and practices to leadership, reconciles languages of design and business and weaves them together, making both stronger and more resilient. Each language is distinct and important in its own right, but the process of reconciling reminds leaders that their language is not everyone's language; therefore, words (and actions) must be chosen carefully.

Coming back to our three barriers—aimlessness, fear, and illiteracy—it's appropriate to contemplate their potential consequences. Being lost can undermine confidence, fear of change means missing opportunities, and illiteracy may mean that we mismanage even those opportunities that we notice and pursue.

If we are to deal with these problems, we must change the way we learn. We must strive to understand—and reform—the way we work alone, the opportunities we have to collaborate

"If students aren't taught the language of sound and images, shouldn't they be considered as illiterate as if they left college without being able to read or write?"

FILMMAKER GEORGE LUCAS, INTERVIEW IN *EDUTOPIA*, SEPTEMBER 2004

with others, and the responsibility we have to lead. These challenges demand designed leadership, propelled by the strategic design principles and methods.

What follows is a guide to designed leadership, in two parts: designed leadership principles and method (the theory) and designed leadership learning and practice. The book is written for people who like to sample books, so you can move in and out of sections and chapters at will.

In the following pages, I explore the integration of design and leadership—unpacking the principles, methods, and practices of strategic design, then translating and applying them to business, government, academia, and civil society. To the degree that you can incorporate these into your own skill set, they will make your efforts—and those of the people around you—more successful, whatever the pursuit.

You will find a translation of built-environment design principles into a "ways of thinking" tool kit that builds the bridge between theory and practice. I also explore ways to practice designed leadership by thinking visually and spatially in places like studios. The idea that designed leadership is about learning deserves its own chapter. Finally, I recount a series of frontline leadership stories that ground the principles and practices in hard-learned leadership lessons.

This book is about how we can lead better. As we remember the joys and potential of lifelong learning, it is also worth remembering that the leaders among us, from every sector, all once faced the world as fresh-faced, wide-eyed, and innocent preschoolers—yet to become the welder, the postdoctoral fellow, the executive, the in-home worker, the cabinetmaker, the cabinet minister, or the member of Congress. The principles here will connect the surviving naïfs in us all to the disciplined future leaders that we all have the capacity to become.

PART I

Principles and Methods

IN THIS SECTION I lay the foundation for understanding the principles and methods of designed leadership.

In chapter 1, I write about the importance of core, process, and foundation values. I then outline ten principles of designed leadership that are based on the strategic design method—a collaborative, visual, disciplined thinking method for tackling complex problems (small and large) and systemic challenges.

These ten principles ideally illuminate how a designer mindset applies to leadership and can be useful to employ in life and work.

1. Make Values Explicit
2. Know Place and Experience
3. Value Diversity

4. Emphasize Edges and Boundaries
5. Bridge Gaps and Make Connections
6. Evaluate for Fit, Scale, and Context
7. Learn from Natural Systems
8. Apply the Jane Jacobs Test
9. Attend to Patterns
10. Never Finished but Always Complete

In chapter 2 I dive into the strategic design method, explaining ASK, TRY, DO, and giving a simple "design an adventure weekend" example of how to use the method. I provide a reference list of techniques for each of the ASK, TRY, and DO processes that I use in the example.

I

Ten Principles for Designed Leadership

"Management is doing things right; leadership is doing the right things."

—PETER F. DRUCKER, *ESSENTIAL DRUCKER: MANAGEMENT, THE INDIVIDUAL AND SOCIETY*, 2001

"The man who grasps principles can successfully select his own methods. The man who tries methods, ignoring principles, is sure to have trouble."

—HARRINGTON EMERSON, *THE TWELVE PRINCIPLES OF EFFICIENCY*, 1912

A Matter of Principle

PRINCIPLE IS JUST a word adrift. In one system, principles bridge values and practices—a principle is a statement to clarify a value in application.[1] By that definition, principles are not instinctive but learned. For most people, however, there is less thought and more passion behind their unspoken principles. Design is a principled decision-making process; designed leadership is a principled learning process.

A Question of Value

"Designed" is a *value*. Intentional. Disciplined. Fun. Everyone has values, yet few people use normative identifiers to describe their thinking or conduct. A colleague, for example, starts by assuming that people are selfish, arrogant, argumentative, ungrateful, fickle, pretenders and dissemblers, evaders of danger, and eager for gain; he is inspired by how we learn to be respectful, cooperative, collaborative, and effective.[2] Values are tough to articulate, and even more difficult to pay attention to when we should.

"*Design*" itself is a protean word that can be a noun, an adjective, or a verb. As a noun, it too is a value—really, a *meta-value* that needs to be couched by qualifiers like "good," or "effective," or "modern," that clarify intended qualities. As an adjective or verb, design can either modify a "process" or be a process itself.

Using Values Intentionally

In designed leadership, values are strategic markers to orient principles and provide touchstones for assessments of incremental or final performance. This accountability (also a value) is fundamental to the effectiveness of designed leadership—it's the value-add of the design process generally. Together with David Fushtey, governance lawyer, I have sketched a diagram called "Designed by Intent," indicating core values, process values, and foundation values that all interact with one another and demand reconciliation.[3] We like the idea of intention, knowing that design is driven to move well beyond talking toward concrete action.

Core Values

Core values are those values (such as accountability, effectiveness, elegance, and respect) that are defined only as a means to aggregate other components or meta-values.

Accountability. In many of the governance structures I have inherited, there have been accountability gaps. Even for the deeply ethical, accountability can be a tricky concept. In many countries, the word is associated only with financial or numeric accounting. However, we cannot assume that we all understand this word the same way. Thanks to my own professional practice, I have come to a clear definition.[4] Despite the criticality of accountability in relationships and leadership positions, there exists a clarity gap around my responsibilities and my accountability.

Effectiveness. It is hard to imagine an organization that doesn't value and reward effectiveness. The problem, again, is in understanding what effectiveness means to the engineer, the politician, the academic, the financier, the native citizen, and the global citizen. Accountability is oversight and assessment by outside parties. Effectiveness, to me, is the assessment of internal values. Effectiveness ranges from relationships to communication to process understanding to getting the job done.

Elegance. Elegant solutions are different for different people, but the value and principles should be the same. The mathematician, the computer programmer, the haute couture designer, and the diplomat all respect that an elegant outcome is one that takes complex inputs and makes the solution look easy. Solutions to difficult-to-define, not-one-right-answer problems[5] can be deliciously elegant, achieved through hard work and intention. In good design, elegance is enduring. Elegant solutions look simple, succinct, even understated.

Respect. Of all the values, respect is core, process, and foundation all rolled together for designed leadership. It is essential, aspirational, and learned. Only with respect can you successfully navigate hundreds of belief systems, thousands of languages, and billions of experiences. Now, more than ever, people have to feel respected before they can be comfortable with change, and these days change is constant. Again, strategic design demands that we ask questions, and one of the best ways to show respect is to listen—carefully and actively, with full attention. When things have gone off track during a change process, I've generally recognized that it was because I had not listened carefully or communicated consistently. The most resistant person or response will provide an insight that is useful and can move an idea ahead. Respect is why it is important to plan for deliberative processes—for effective, elegant, and accountable outcomes.

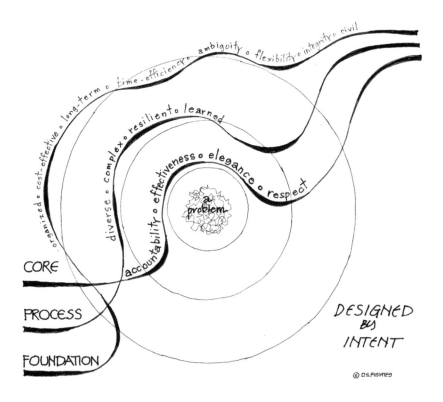

Process Values

Complexity, resilience, diversity, erudition—these values bring another perspective to intentional design. Process values help direct us and provide guidance through any thinking and problem-solving methodology.

Complexity. Complicated problems can usually be unpacked and systematically solved—they are not easy to solve, but it is doable. Complex problems, on the other hand, can stymie us. They are difficult to define, grapple with, and resolve. If we try to oversimplify, we get into trouble. The strategic design method is intended to be useful for both the complicated and the complex.

Resilience. A good process needs to be nimble and tough. It can't get bogged down in detail or stuck in ambiguity. The resilience of the strategic design method is one of its great strengths—it is adaptable and robust.

Diversity. A good process encourages diversity at every level—welcoming a range of players, thinking modes, media, and techniques. It generally results in a set of dissimilar solution options which contribute to the best solution in the end.

Erudition. Every solution-seeking process has learning embedded within it. The strategic design method is a learning process shaped by asking questions, answering them, and continuing to ask more.

Foundation Values

Working through core values and process values, I realized that there are also foundation values: being organized, honest, intentional, long-term, cost-effective, efficient, and practical. The need for diverse thinking skills like fluency (generating a large number of ideas) and flexibility (generating a variety of types of ideas) is foundational to designed leadership.[6] The purpose of stating

From a First-Nations Economic Plan in the Pacific Northwest, to a Danish big pharma company on the Baltic, the message that **Everything Matters** is being repeated around the world from different traditions, but for common futures.[7]

values clearly is to be able to test and assess performance outcomes against what is a complex matrix of interests and values.

Today, in value terms, everything matters. Designed leadership acknowledges this fact as it encourages you to consider all sides of the problem you are trying to solve.

Ten Designed Leadership Principles

Principles inform our thinking. They are the foundation for taking values into designed leadership practice. For some, principles are beliefs. For others, they are a philosophy for life. For me, they are guidelines to help turn values and ideas into accountable actions.[8]

These principles illuminate how a designer mindset applies to leadership and what principles are useful to apply in life and work.

Becoming self-aware of the reasons behind my leadership decisions has brought me to these ten principles. They come mainly from built-environment theory, but some are informed by my work and research in the public realm.

Principle 1. Make Values Explicit
Make values explicit to communicate more consistently with others in decision making, oversight, and accountability assessments.

Principle 2. Know Place and Experience

Place and experience provide context for decisions, actions, and questioning whether to celebrate, ignore, or change our experiences. But to do any of these with informed intent, one must find their genius loci. Those who ignore a sense of place miss out on unique and profound opportunities to improve experiences, both collective and individual.

Principle 3. Value Diversity

In a global marketplace, diversity brings richness and resilience, and reduces your risk-management profile. Valuing diversity begins by asking, "Is this a good move for people: for that person, that child, that new citizen, that senior citizen, and that visitor?"

Principle 4. Emphasize Edges and Boundaries

Edges and boundaries are rich for analysis, ideas, and not-so-obvious solutions.

Principle 5. Bridge Gaps and Make Connections

It is easy to get comfortable with a vocational vocabulary and isolated communities of interests. It takes intention to bridge gaps and make connections. One vehicle for doing so is the opportune interconnection of the academic, business, government, and civil society sectors.

(CONTINUED NEXT PAGE)

(CONTINUED FROM PREVIOUS PAGE)

Principle 6. Evaluate for Fit, Scale, and Context

Fitting a leader to an organization or an organization to a community is like fitting a house to the land: we can merge, claim, confront, or surround. Scale and context matter.

Principle 7. Learn from Natural Systems

The interconnectivity of natural systems can guide thoughtful, active designed leadership by mirroring their integrated, elegant complexity and amazing functionality. Nature has a million patterns worth emulating, which can serve as tangible examples of designed leadership principles in practice.

Principle 8. Apply the Jane Jacobs Test

Active designed leadership should meet and excel in the Jane Jacob's test: interconnected thinking and doing; mixing and meshing methods; building a density of ideas; and applying focus.

Principle 9. Attend to Patterns

At a strategic level, design identifies information patterns. In the process of reconciling different values and interests, those patterns are deconstructed and reconstructed in different ways. This skill is learned. Most leaders learn to quickly identify and assess a narrow band of patterns. Designed leadership, by definition, looks at everything, so it is important to use the broadest criteria for distinguishing patterns. It is critical to take note of time, use, materials, cost, risk, people, plants, and animals when seeking to improve or reconstruct.

Principle 10. Never Finished but Always Complete

Designed leadership is never finished, but is always complete and accountable to the values and practical functions requested. The quest for perfection should never end, but neither should it circumvent the delivery of something that is excellent in the present moment.

PRINCIPLE 1: MAKE VALUES EXPLICIT

"The authentic and pure values—truth, beauty, and goodness—in the activity of a human being are the result of one and the same act, a certain application of the full attention to the object."

—SIMONE WEIL, *GRAVITY AND GRACE*, 1948

When I reflect on my various leadership experiences, I realize that each new venture began with a redefinition of values—my own and those of the organization. When I arrived at the executive table at the British Columbia Ministry of Advanced Education,

I asked what their values were. Multiple values were well enumerated in the ministry strategic plan, but there were too many to remember. They were not used when making decisions. As a result, we designed a process to identify the essential values. We landed on respect as the most important value for our decision making. We then clustered four other values of key importance: Integrity, Balance, Learning, and Excellence.

In the world of designed leadership, values are essential underpinnings for key principles and practices. At the ministry, we tried various ways of integrating these values into our decision-making processes, including making them an explicit part of the agenda. This involved cocreating the agenda at the beginning of our meetings and keeping visual reminders around the meeting table. It also required discipline on behalf of the executive to connect our discussions and decisions to our values.

Good designed leadership makes values explicit, stating them in easy-to-understand terms, followed by principles and, often, by guidelines or standards. This way, the values are connected and can be used transparently and openly to inform decision-making.

Designed leadership demands elasticity of thinking—being able to take a value like "respect" and articulate what it means to be respectful, as well as what it means to be disrespectful. This type of discussion helps us more deeply understand values and what they mean.

Another technique for understanding values comes from the Strategic Design Toolkit found on the UBC Sauder d.studio website.[9]

Assumption Dumption[10] can be used to make unstated beliefs explicit, develop shared understanding across diverse groups, explore the problems "behind" the problem, and identify opportunities for further research. It involves asking participants to state their assumptions about a situation or problem and prompts them to reverse these assumptions to see if new opportunities are revealed. Reversing assumptions gives teams a fresh perspective on ideas, values, and beliefs—not unlike standing on one's head! This activity also tends to generate rich discussion that helps team members understand each other's points of view and explore the origins of the group's beliefs. This unpacking of assumptions helps the team dive more deeply into the problem to discover its true source.

Assumption Dumption is an exercise that helps unpack values in any problem or opportunity.

A specific question is posed to your client, team, or sometimes to yourself: What are the assumptions that you hold about this problem? We asked senior officials in a ministry of health, "What assumptions do members of the public hold about your ministry?" One of the responses was that people assume the government (e.g., the ministry of health) will look after them in their old age. Given the costs of healthcare, this is a faulty assumption, and the process reveals a number of questions that need answers. Reversing the assumption is also useful: What happens if people are instructed from kindergarten that we have to look after ourselves and cannot depend on the government?

As we unpack assumptions, we discover unspoken values and trigger a diversity of questions that need to be asked and answered as part of problem scoping. Just as the strategic design method demands that we make values explicit, designed leadership requires that leaders discuss their values openly for decision making. Questioning assumptions is good reflective practice. Have we correctly identified the values at play? Are we aligned with the values that we articulated as part of the solution-seeking process? And have we sufficiently communicated our inner thinking process in a language that everyone can understand?

The novelist John Lanchester wrote humorously about the challenges of learning the language of finance. He uses the example of the "hedge" or "hedge fund." As a term for setting limits on a bet, a hedge was a clever way for gamblers to delimit the size of their potential losses, "just as a real hedge delimits the size of a field."[11] Physical turned metaphorical turned technical. "And that is the story of how a hedge, setting a limit to a field, became what it is today: a largely unregulated pool of private capital, often using enormous amounts of leverage and borrowing to multiply the size of its bets. This is reversification in its full glory."[12]

Language is always challenging when communicating values—especially in the integration of design and business. Your average arbitrage specialist may have no clue about the meaning of "ideogram" (a written character symbolizing an idea).

When we cross disciplines and start talking business and design, spoken and written language is at the root of both the problem and the opportunity. We may have access to the universal language of images, but how often is the access to images guarded by key words?

Hugh Dubberly, a design thought leader, writes this about language and organizations: "Language is the defining environment in which [these] systems live. It is how those in the system reach agreement. It is also a medium for organization growth and change."[13] I think the same is true about the effect of design processes and the potential effect of design language on leadership. Language is the medium we use to explore and learn, to grow and change—based on our values. So, connecting the languages of business and the language of design has the potential to create new language and new behavior—and, ideally, new approaches to problem solving.

It is vitally important to clarify your own values, and to work with colleagues to define the key values of a community or organization. Once defined, it is important to use values in decision making and strategic thinking.

Principle 1: Make values explicit, communicate them, and use them in decision making.

PRINCIPLE 2: KNOW PLACE AND EXPERIENCE

"Away up there in Pendrell Sound,
Were three little sea-gals floating on a log,
Don't you scare us,
They shouted as they flew into the air.
Oh, bother, it's only Moura's father,
And they all sat down on the water."

—DANIEL BRANCH QUAYLE, LETTER TO AUTHOR, 1956

"People never learn anything by being told, they have to find out for themselves."

— PAULO COELHO, *VERONIKA DECIDES TO DIE: A NOVEL OF REDEMPTION*, 1999

"Nothing ever becomes real till it is experienced. Even a proverb is no proverb to you till your Life [sic] has illustrated it."

—JOHN KEATS, LETTER TO GEORGE AND GEORGIANA KEATS, FEBRUARY 14, 1819

Knowing Place

Knowing place has to do with our comfort in the various environments that we inhabit on a daily basis—especially our home and our workplace.

The geographer Anne Buttimer (1980) has described our relationship to place as an exchange between home and horizons of reach. Home embodies our desire for rest, territory, security, community. Horizons of reach represent movement, range, adventure, innovation. . . . When the home and reach of our imaginations and our social affiliations are fulfilled in the place where we live, we enjoy centered lives. Often, however, what we desire to be and the people we desire to be with conflict with where we are.[14]

I didn't begin to understand my own place in the world until I was removed from my home landscape—first to central Canada and then to the Bay Area in California. The product of a small town on Vancouver Island on the Pacific Coast of Canada, I moved in the early eighties to attend graduate school at the University of California, Berkeley. What I found was a different Berkeley from the one that had flourished in the sixties, or even the seventies: it was calmer and strangely preppy. I attended while Clare Cooper-Marcus, now a professor emerita recognized for her research on the social and psychological implications of design, taught a popular graduate course called Social Factors in Design. One assignment required us to write our environmental autobiography.[15] We wrote

about the places and experiences that shaped us from our earliest memories through adolescence and into adulthood. I remember my friend Valerie writing about how profoundly influential the car was during her teenage years in California, and thinking how different her memory was from my own experience in small town Vancouver Island. We can learn a great deal about the culture of places and organizations through these kinds of reflections.

When I started teaching at the University of British Columbia, I translated the environmental autobiography assignment to make it my own, which became a mainstay in my teaching. The primary goal of writing an environmental autobiography is to increase self-awareness. Through the process, one gains understanding, sensitivity, and respect for each unique environmental history. It is clearly useful for design students who need to be aware of their values and biases as they design spaces and places for others. I would argue that it is equally useful for our roles as leaders because it illuminates a personal awareness of the context in which leaders think and eventually make decisions or decide on directions.

I am four years old and my mother is showing me a letter from my father. My dad, a passionate marine biologist of the bivalve mollusk persuasion (clams and oysters to us), spent most of the summers in those days on a raft in the place called Pendrell Sound, looking through a microscope. Pendrell Sound happens to have the ideal water temperature and salinity to grow baby oysters. My father would write letters, in pencil, with drawings of the animals of Pendrell Sound. He would append their Latin names, like the shore crab, *Hemigrapsus*. My introduction to nature was therefore both academic and experiential.

Our roots and experiences shape us one way or another. I consider myself an urban person. I am virtually allergic to

Hello, Moura

Gasfy the stickle back.
There are quite a few
of them near my float.
Pretty soon they all be having babies. They
have sharp spines just like a rose bush.

Baldy the
eagle.

Baldy lives on the
island near my tent.
He's a big bird with a
white head, a white tail.
He catches fish in his
sharp claws and takes
them to the shore where
he eats them. Once in a
while 2 or 3 crows chase
and tease him – but
I don't think he gets
really angry; jus annoyed.

I got the last letter you wrote, thank
you. Be sure and write me next time, too,
please. As soon as the baby oysters
grow up I'll be back to see you.
Bye –Daddy.

camping, and I get more excited by the city than by the countryside. That being said, my discipline is landscape architecture,
which makes nature an important part of my life. I love nature
in the city—the rough and the refined. Without nature, the city
isn't what it can or should be. This conundrum of dialectics

or opposites—urban/rural, inside/outside, tamed/wild—permeates my life and propels me to engage these dualities in my design work, my academic work, and my work shaping cities and leadership.

Designed leadership is about being grounded in both our geographic and psychological place and knowing how we fit into those places. It is about the continual search for our place—which can change our lives as leaders. *New York Times* contributor Pamela Druckerman understands this implicitly. She caught my attention when she wrote:
"A few guidelines for creative people: First, stay in the room. And don't fill those moments with cat videos." Druckerman was asked to deliver a commencement address to graduating students at Sciences Po in Paris. She decided to base her talk on a common French expression: *Vous allez trouver votre place*. You will find your place. She said, "I've always liked this idea that, somewhere in the world, there's a gap shaped just like you. Once you find it, you'll slide right in."

Druckerman asks an important question: How do we find that place? She offers great advice, especially to what she calls "creative types": "Stay in the room. It needn't be an actual room. You can be alone in a busy café," and, "You need to be blank, and even a little bit bored, for your brain to feed you ideas."

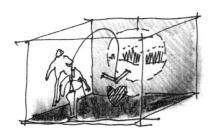

Druckerman also provides advice about time management, idea recording, and our productivity: "Figure out your clearest, most productive time of day to work, and guard this time carefully. Always carry a pen, a paper notebook, and something good to read."[16]

Instead of forming ideas of who and what we are on the basis of a found identity that is fixed by social role or tradition, we begin to understand ourselves in terms of a made identity that is constructed (and frequently reconstructed) out of many cultural sources.

Awareness of our environmental autobiography and the continual search for the gap shaped to fit us are part of the dynamic of designed leadership.

Knowing Experience

Our environmental experiences, from infancy into childhood, are profoundly influential in shaping our view of the world and our sense of respect for people and environment. "Natural environments, for example, have been 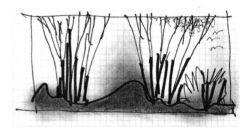 repeatedly shown to have the capacity to bring out the best in people even when nature is no more than the view of a tree from a window."[17]

Children's experiences can teach them about the importance of place in their lives. For example, natural landscapes that children adopt as their own give them a sense of privacy, autonomy, and control.

From the designed-leadership perspective, leaders, too, need a sense of their place loaded with experience. Having a child's view of the world can lend a special sense of our own place, especially in thinking about the short-term and long-term effects of our decisions and the solutions they create.

Child culture is full of rituals and rules with important meanings. Children have a secret life—a distinctive history formed away from adult eyes. Christopher Robin says it all in A. A. Milne's "Solitude,"[18] explaining the sense of children being able, in their secret space, to redesign the world—empowering them to create their own counterculture and play out conflicts which they might observe in the adult milieu.

Such experiences are the platform for our adult understanding of experience and place. As adults, we move on from our childhood experiences and forget to think about them and their lasting power.

In the world of built environment design, the concept of opposites—also referred to in terms of dualities and dialectics—is important for deriving meaning from and explaining experience. Recognizing dualities and their dialectics can guide a built-environment designer to make certain decisions about space and place and can similarly guide a strategic designer to think carefully about an organizational or leadership challenge in these terms.

Douglas Paterson, eminent thinker on the theories of landscape experience, wrote and taught about the importance of dualities and dialectics in our lives, especially as we experience spaces and places. As Paterson explains: "The existence of these opposite conditions requires constant attention and resolution. When confronted with *disorder* in a space around us, we seek to define an *order* to facilitate our passage through the landscape. When confronted with too much order, we intentionally seek *disorder* as a form of amusement or relaxation."[19]

In the spirit of speculation, I have taken some of Paterson's ideas and linked them to designed leadership.[20]

"Good" designed leadership both reflects and generates shared images. The leader understands the dominant "opposite" conditions in their organization (public/ private, top-down/bottom-up, in-the-know/out-of-the-know), which explain the culture and the experience of his/her colleagues in that place. This understanding makes it more likely for an individual to resolve conflicts, create new ideas, and foster opportunities for shared experiences.

"Good" designed leadership possesses an endless number of experiences. The idea here is that more is better. The more "oppositional" conditions that leadership holds, the better the leadership. Better because of the clarity that comes from explaining the dualities in the course of any set of decisions or daily activities: conscious/unconscious, simplicity /complexity, clarity/ambiguity, public/private, sacred/profane, foreign /familiar, free/constrained, complete/incomplete, fixed/moveable.

Using the oppositional conditions clarifies critical debate. Generating questions around these dialectic conditions can be the focus of debate and discussion in a leadership team or an organization 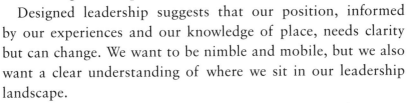 as a whole. The exploration of dualities is another way to generate questions during the Ask phase of any process.

Designed leadership suggests that our position, informed by our experiences and our knowledge of place, needs clarity but can change. We want to be nimble and mobile, but we also want a clear understanding of where we sit in our leadership landscape.

Principle 2: To know both place and experience is to have context for decisions and actions. It is about our genius loci, finding our place and finding ourselves.

PRINCIPLE 3: VALUE DIVERSITY

"When I think about diversity, I actually think about the word 'inclusion.' And I think this is a time of great inclusion. It's not men, it's not women alone. Whether it's geographic, it's approach, it's your style, it's your way of learning, the way you want to contribute, it's your age—it is really broad."

—GINNI ROMETTY, CHAIR AND CEO OF IBM, INTERVIEW IN *FORTUNE*, OCTOBER 2, 2012

"There is no safe depository of the ultimate powers of society but the people themselves; and if we think them not enlightened enough to exercise their control with a wholesome discretion, the remedy is not to take it from them, but to inform their discretion."

—THOMAS JEFFERSON, LETTER TO WILLIAM CHARLES JARVIS, SEPTEMBER 28, 1820

The world would be a different place if global leaders, city councilors, and village mayors used the following questions when making decisions: Is this good for children? Is it good for the elderly? Is it good for the disabled? It is unfortunate that we neglect to fully consider a diverse population in our decision- and policy-making processes.

The same thing might be true for businesses and for leadership. What if leaders made decisions through the diversity lens? It would mean taking the long view. First Nations in Canada and indigenous peoples globally embrace the idea that we need to be planning for seven generations into the future. This is a good principle for designed leadership. It would also mean thinking differently about the present—about safety, security, and well-being. It might even mean that there should be more play, fun, and laughter in the workplace.

The earth does not belong to man, man belongs to the earth.
All things are connected like the blood that unites one family.
Man did not weave the web of life, he is merely a strand in it.
Whatever he does to the web, he does to himself.
The earth is sacred and men and animals are but one part of it.

—EXCERPT FROM CHIEF SEATTLE

Designed leadership allows you to go to a child's place or a senior's place, to think like one of them, play like one of them, and come back to your world better positioned to make clear and valuable decisions.

People are important in any design project—whether it be product design, built-environment design, or strategic design. The principle of valuing diversity emphasizes knowing about the experiences that customers have in stores and online. Learning how to step into the shoes of other people is an essential skill.

Despite a disproportionate amount of design literature claiming that the origin of a human-centric approach to design lies with computer science and artificial intelligence, other design disciplines, like built-environment design, have always held the user as the most important player in the design process.[21]

Still, we can never be reminded enough to focus on people and diversity. Back in 2009, IDEO, the best design marketers in the world, created the *HCD Toolkit*—a book that explained the importance of human-centered design in the social sector. As they note, "A community of designers, entrepreneurs, and social sector innovators embrace it, buying and downloading over 150,000 copies."[22]

The point of this principle is to accept the obvious importance of human-centered design, and to ensure that this means a range of people—by age, ethnicity, demographics, and capacities.

The strategic design mindset, and therefore designed leadership, is all about stepping into someone else's shoes and seeing their perspective.

Principle 3: Valuing diversity means asking, "Is this a good move for people—for children, seniors, the disabled?"

PRINCIPLE 4: EMPHASIZE EDGES
AND BOUNDARIES

"To push the boundaries, you need to know where the edges are."

—MARK BOULTON, IN *DESIGNING FOR THE WEB*, 2009

"I want to stay as close to the edge as I can without going over. Out on the edge, you see all kinds of things you can't see from the center."

—ED FINNERTY, IN *PLAYER PIANO* BY KURT VONNEGUT, JR., 1971

Edges come in all shapes, types, and sizes. Some physical edges are crisp, like where different materials meet in a building—window glass meets windowsill. Edges of furniture can be beveled or rounded, so they don't upset the back of our knees when we sit in a chair. Some edges are miles long, like the ocean's shore, where water meets land. Other edges are jagged and frightening, like broken glass. We have fuzzy edges (unmowed grass meets mowed grass) and transitional edges (where one thing begins and another thing ends).

Boundaries, too, mean many things. Boundaries can be edges. They can separate countries, an in or out tennis shot, or they can represent the scope of a topic for an essay (or a book).

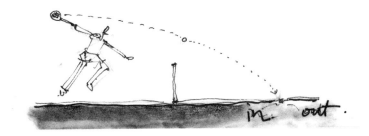

In nature, edges and boundaries tend to be where you find most of the action. In weather systems, it's where you find the storms. In biological habitats, it's where you find the most biodiversity. Edges in the landscape are the richest in animal and plant life. They are also visually rich—they provide us with differing textures, smells, tastes, and experiences. When the forest meets the marsh—now that is an edge to reckon with. But this sounds like a landscape architect talking. Edges and boundaries are also relevant to designed leadership.

In the world of designed leadership, edges and boundaries are important to problem scoping, finding meaning, and finding opportunities.

Problem Scoping

Scoping a problem is one of the most difficult challenges in the strategic design method. It is so much easier just to accept whatever problem we are given and take a run at solving it. This tends to be a habit—learned early in our lives—that gives the appearance of efficiency and effectiveness. And it is a modus operandi that works for some problems—generally the really simple ones. But as problems get more complex and ill-defined, scoping is essential.

By scoping, I mean unpacking the problem into its various components—looking at it from all sides and upside down.

We explore the problem space and see where the edges are, and how to describe their characteristics. Some problems seem boundary-less and edge-less. The challenge is how to combine edges and boundaries in a way that visually helps us scope a problem, unpack it, and see its edges—fuzzy or clear.

Finding Facts, Finding Meaning

Finding facts is about gathering objective data. Finding meaning is about interpreting and synthesizing those facts, reviewing them and then identifying chunks of the problem or opportunity that are small enough to solve.

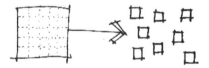

Enter edges and boundaries. Researching and asking questions pushes us over the edge. Information needs to be examined and questioned to see if it belongs. It is also useful to visually map the facts we find. Sometimes the context is just too big to grapple with. In that case, it's good to synthesize and reduce the scope—in essence, to make the edges more crisp and less fuzzy. We need to think about the context and allow ourselves to change scales as we think about a problem—inside and outside of the predetermined boundary. Or we give ourselves instructions to constantly and consciously change the boundaries. By focusing on edges, those "almost-in/almost-out" areas of a problem, we gain different perspectives.

It can be difficult to move from finding facts, or the observations about any given problem, to finding meaning or gaining insight. Therefore, after exploring the edge and beyond the boundary, it is necessary to focus. Finding the center of the problem and mapping its relative proximity to the edges and boundaries can then be more fruitful. The facts are presented in a new context.

Finding Opportunities

Boundaries and edges can play the same role in seeking opportunities. They help us take the problem apart, to find bite-sized chunks that we can tackle without being overwhelmed. If we set the boundary and edge as a smaller, manageable problem, it helps us learn about the bigger, more complex problem.

Boundaries and edges can also help us defer judgment. By this I mean delaying the speedy drive to solution—holding back and asking questions, wondering about whether the boundary or edge is in the right place for this opportunity.

Clarifying the boundary also helps us determine criteria for the success of our eventual solution. We can use boundaries and edges to keep reframing our problems and opportunities to see them in different ways. As Vonnegut suggests, we can use the edge as a perch, a way of seeing beyond the horizon, to remind us to continually expand and contract our context.

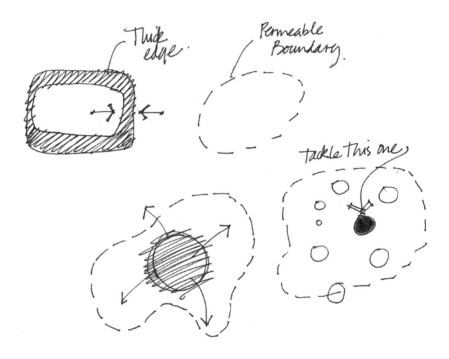

Edges and boundaries as concepts are useful to remind us that the strategic design method is continuous and iterative. Running around the edge of a circle, for example, means that you'll come back to where you started; you can check in and see whether you are still on track.

Principle 4: Edges and boundaries are places of richness for analysis, ideas, and not-so-obvious solutions.

PRINCIPLE 5: BRIDGE GAPS AND MAKE CONNECTIONS

"The great enemy of communication, we find, is the illusion of it. We have talked enough; but we have not listened. And by not listening we have failed to concede the immense complexity of our society—and thus the great gaps between ourselves and those with whom we seek understanding."

—WILLIAM H. WHYTE, IN *FORTUNE*, SEPTEMBER 1950

"Solitude is out of fashion. Our companies, our schools and our culture are in thrall to an idea I call the New Groupthink, which holds that creativity and achievement come from an oddly gregarious place. Most of us now work in teams, in offices without walls, for managers who prize people skills above all. Lone geniuses are out. Collaboration is in."

—SUSAN CAIN, IN *THE NEW YORK TIMES*, JANUARY 13, 2012

Susan Cain, the author of *Quiet: The Power of Introverts in a World That Can't Stop Talking*, captures the challenge of achieving balance: most of us need time alone and time in groups.[23] Groupthink can be dangerous because it keeps us in a place that is comfortable—especially if we are in a group where we all reinforce one another's ideas, places, and positions in the world. The idea is to bring as many sectors as possible into the process: academia, business, government, and civil society. The rationale is that if we listen to all sectors, there is a much better chance that we will arrive at a solution or a way forward that is workable, practical, and maybe even creative.

Embedded in the concept of how the sectors relate and work together is the challenge of learning from one another. There is a worldwide explosion of interest in the question of how contemporary societies might strengthen the connections between research and evidence on the one hand, and policy and practice on the other.[24] Given the various gaps that exist in our capacity to work together and exchange information for better decision making, the "working across sectors" concept has the potential to bridge those gaps.

Bridging the Gaps

Strategic design is about stepping back, laying out what you know, and then asking questions to help identify the gaps. Gap analyses are common practice: where are we, and where do we want to be? The idea is not to dwell on the gap itself, but to build a bridge to get to the other side.

However, it is instructive in the strategic design method to review the kinds of gaps that we encounter. There are a variety of common gaps: communication and literacy gaps, theory and practice gaps, cultural gaps, governance and resources gaps, and knowledge mobilization gaps.

Communication and Literacy Gaps

Formal communication mechanisms are often missing between the generators of knowledge (researchers) and public servants thirsty for information to provide evidence-based policy. A similar gap exists in the relationships between business and government. For example, it is difficult for businesses to articulate particular public policy challenges, and sometimes equally difficult for governments to understand these challenges. Academics, businesspeople, public servants, and civil society all speak different languages. It takes time to build a shared vocabulary, to respectfully listen to each other, and to learn together. Frequently, the successful bridging of these gaps rests on building relationships between people.

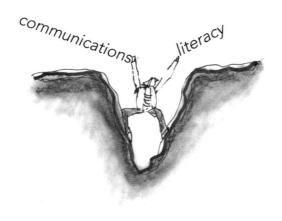

Theory/Practice Gaps

Access to information is crucial, as is confidence in that information, its usefulness, and the capacity to use it in practice. For instance, how is theoretical business research translated to be understood and used by business? How do business researchers ask business leaders what information/data is needed to contribute to the new economy, or to a business context that is ever-changing? This gap was also revealed in the dot-com bust, which demonstrated a significant breakdown in terms of the availability of useful information in the business community, or the lack of trust about that information when businesses are making decisions.

Cultural Gaps

Academia tends to foster a culture of competitiveness, although there are signs of change in the reward system to encourage more collaboration. Similarly, in government, relationship building and collaboration are challenging. Businesses also thrive in a competitive environment, but more leaders are acknowledging that collaboration, at least within organizations, is essential. Ideally, the academy would make sure that people entering the business world have the skills to work in a collaborative environment. As well, there has to be more encouragement for savvy new employees to be productively disruptive—to innovate within the business culture.

Governance and Resources Gaps

One of the many challenges in developing any kind of cross-sectoral collaborative model is developing a funding and governance model that works for all parties. Getting these right can be the difference between a bridging success and a bridging failure.

Knowledge Mobilization Gaps

There are significant gaps between knowledge producers (generally professors in academia), inventors and innovators (generally businesses, with some academia), and knowledge consumers (generally government, business, and civil society). These knowledge mobilization gaps or the lack of communication among the sectors impede our capacity to make better decisions, especially in the world of policy design and development.

An example of a multisectoral designed leadership experiment is the campus-city collaborative started in the City of Vancouver as part of the *Greenest City Action Plan.*[25] One of the strategies connected the universities in the city with the city government itself. There were two ideas that drove the initial concept: (1) preparing students at our postsecondary institutions for "green jobs;" and (2) utilizing relevant research from universities to help achieve the greenest city targets (zero waste, district energy systems to power individual neighborhoods). The CityStudio grew out of this experiment—a successful collaboration involving postsecondary institutions, neighborhoods, city staff and businesses—that engages students in work-ready learning while making improvements to their city. See chapter 6 for more details on the campus-city collaborative and an example of bridging multisectoral gaps.

Designed leadership can help bridge these gaps—or at least help us think about them differently. The goal is to strike an appropriate balance between large-scale evidence and local contexts, diversity and complexities.[26]

Principle 5: Make connections and bridge gaps through engaging academia, business, government, nongovernment, and civil society throughout any process.

PRINCIPLE 6: EVALUATE FOR FIT, SCALE, AND CONTEXT

Charles Moore, the Californian architect, is perhaps best known for Sea Ranch, a housing community sited on the windy and dramatic Sonoma coastline. Alexandra Lange describes Sea Ranch:

"The combination of timelessness and whimsy, landscape form and antic decoration, made the Sea Ranch highly photogenic and instantly influential."[27]

Moore, a writer, teacher, and asker of great questions, consistently ponders the importance of place. He wonders what it means to make a place and what it means to have people inhabit that place. At the same time, he is equally captivated by questions of "fit," and not just by what  element of the built environment might tuck most comfortably into the landscape. He also digs into the tensions between democracy and private land ownership, as well as the concern around how we make places that work for public life.[28]

But, as Jamer Hunt might argue, finding a good fit requires more than the identification of a single, isolated niche. We must also consider scale and context. I first encountered Hunt at the 2015 Future of Innovation Summit in Como, Italy, a fascinating international contemplation on the intersection of innovation, big data, and behavioral economics.[29] Hunt, a professor at Parsons School of Design, shared his own explorations of the idea of scale and its importance to how we view the world, and how we propose to change it for the better.[30] He also introduced a scalar framing exercise based on Eames' "Power of 10," 10^1 being the scale of the human body (the bicycle); 10^2 the streets we ride bicycles on (urban design); 10^3 neighborhoods (architectural/landscape level); 10^4 regional scale (systems integration), and so on. His message was that scale really frames the problem.

That is certainly the case in any organization. What is the scale of the endeavor? And if scale is so important, how is it connected to context? In some ways, I think of scale and context as being complementary. If scale is the definitive "size" of whatever we are working with (the three-person startup or the thirty-thousand-person corporation), context is more descriptive—it goes beyond the quantitative size of something into the qualitative description. Both are important. But first to explore "fit."

In *Place of Houses*, Charles Moore notes four ways to fit a house into the landscape:

• Merging: blending the house into the landscape, picking up the cues, such that, "Though it is man-made, [the house] can give the impression of being at one with its surroundings, and consonant with them."[31]

• Claiming: the opposite of merging—the house is a clear and strong shape in contrast to the land around it. "The house seems what it is, man-made and intentionally different from its natural setting."[32] The house has power to claim the land around it.

• Enfronting: buildings with imposing facades "enfront" a part of the land, usually a street or square. "Enfronting the site requires one face of the house to be made special in order to address a certain feature of the site."[33]

• Surrounding: "Elements of the house close around a part of the land to make a private domain outdoors."[34] This can be a partial closure—an intensified version of claiming.

The site and its limitations give us clues about what kind of "fit" to suggest. Culture, geography, landscape type, and climate all play a role.

How does this translate to the fit of leadership to a community? Fit is a great word. Being a fan of one-syllable words (ASK, TRY, DO), the concise "fit" is all-purpose and specific at the same time. It's about the fit of a leader to his or her organization—as well as the fit of the organization to its community.

Using Moore's principles of fit-ness, we can extrapolate the concepts of merging, claiming, enfronting, and surrounding to have meaning in designed leadership.

The leader blends: The leader blends into his or her environment, picking up and using cues like a chameleon, to be as one with the organization. Leadership is subtle and embraces the culture.

The leader claims: This approach is 180 degrees from merging. The leader claims a separate position in the organization, one of prospect and one of difference. The leader uses this position carefully, and occasionally, when a claiming attitude is needed or helpful.

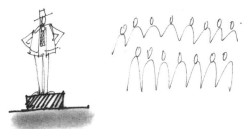

The leader calls attention: The leader creates a purposeful "facade" designed to respond to a particular context or need in the organization. This approach isn't for the long term, it is for a snapshot to enfront an issue and bring it to attention.

The leader engages: While in landscape design this is an extreme version of claiming, in management it can be an extreme of merging. The leader might engage a colleague or a team for the purposes of coaching or mentoring, perhaps bringing focus to how people are working, collaborating, or responding to a particular problem.

The practice of designed leadership demands attention to the concept of fit, being aware of how context changes and being capable of adapting our response. Designed leadership also offers an advantage over built-environment design: if you're building a house, you have only one chance to choose your approach—to merge or claim, to enfront or surround. But a good leader—a leader with a designed leadership lens—can constantly modify his or her approach to fit the occasion.

Back to scale and context. Hunt speculates that the meso-scale is the most important. In the challenge of scaling up an idea, an organization, a movement—it is a balance of top-down and bottom-up. Top-down can be faster, but also holds the risk of not involving the right people; it is process-light. Bottom-up can be slow, but it is responsive, granular, and specific; it is process-heavy. We need both to ensure good results. Back to fit: scale and context are critical.

Principle 6: Fitting a leader to an organization or an organization to a community is like fitting a house to the land: we can merge, claim, enfront, or surround. Scale and context matter.

PRINCIPLE 7: LEARN FROM NATURAL SYSTEMS

"Proceeding calmly, valuing their words
Task accomplished, matter settled
The people all say, 'We did it naturally.'"

—LAOZI, *DAODEJING*, SIXTH CENTURY B.C.

"Uniformity is not nature's way: diversity is nature's way."

—VANDANA SHIVA, INTERVIEW IN *NEW INTERNATIONALIST MAGAZINE*, JUNE 1995

You might wonder what in the world nature has to do with business and leadership. Both are about systems and interconnectivity. Every day we find out more about connections. Every day we find out how interconnected our lives are, and how inextricably linked they are to systems of weather, climate, economy, and health.

We talk about business systems in a way that makes us envision an operating framework. Here is the link to natural systems: they also create a framework for operating. Mother Nature likes to keep things in balance, despite our efforts to the contrary. Designers, especially landscape architects, view the world through the lens of the ecological system. What is connected to what? If I push here, what will happen in the rest of the system?

One of the most powerful books on design theory and ecological systems was written by Michael Hough, a gentle Scot who lived in Toronto, taught at York University, and practiced his profession in the region where he lived, in particular the Don Valley. He wrote about "a language of design for the city whose base rests on the principles of natural process, economy of means, diversity and the enhancement of the environment."[35]

There is a set of principles around how a landscape operates: it rains and the rain goes somewhere—into the ground, into people's basements, into catch basins, and then into the aquifers—and then it comes round again.

If we think about business in the same systemic way, we can discern principles that allow us to understand how change that occurs in one part of the business system will create change in another part. Resilient businesses understand this. Leaders who understand the need for resilience are thinking about systems or thinking in a systemic way.

Natural processes—rain, snow, the seasons—are a part of our lives. Hough writes: "The form of the place reveals its natural and human history and the continuing cycles of natural process."[36] How do we think of businesses and leadership in this way? The form of the business and its history might be important predictors of future cycles. In which case, could studying the evolutionary culture and history of a business reveal much to someone who was trying to understand business model transformation? Understanding the systems, reading them, could be critical in revealing the best ways to disrupt them in the future. Leaders who think about their organizations as a set of interconnected processes make different types of decisions and ask different types of questions.

One of the most important lessons that I learned from Michael was the idea of least effort, or the economy of means. He explained it this way: "The city's used or unwanted materials, its heat energy, garbage and storm water—vacant lands—become useful resources at less environmental and economic cost when the right linkages are established."[37]

"When the right linkages are established"—a reminder to think within the context of the system, to pay attention to the interconnections. From a business and leadership perspective, how do we analyze a problem using the principle of the economy of means? Is there a solution that acknowledges inherent complexity and can repurpose resources that we might otherwise consider useless?

Least effort also translates into "starting change where it is easiest to accomplish" or "modest ambitions" (low-hanging fruit or quick wins). This approach can be particularly useful when you are trying to decide where to engage a community—a workplace or a neighborhood—in considering options for their future. A quick win allows for a sense of accomplishment and a time for reflection about what's next.

Nature also privileges diversity. The healthiest landscape, wild or urban, is the diverse one: whether you are talking about diverse activities, diverse people, or diverse plant and animal life. Diversity is healthy (Principle 3). Hough writes: "Diversity makes social as well as environmental sense in the urban setting."[38] In design terms, this implies interest, pleasure, stimulated senses, and varied landscapes. In leadership and business terms, this implies that leaders should surround themselves with people who think differently than they do. Diversity of thought. Diversity of ways of thinking. Diversity of cultures. Diversity of backgrounds and histories. Diversity of passions.

If natural systems function best when they are well connected, then so do social systems. The Internet and social media have made us all intimately connected, like it or not. These are opportunities and challenges for leadership and business.

What happens when natural systems are overloaded? We are experiencing extreme weather because of climate change and other factors. Similarly, people and their social systems can be overloaded. Tim Harford, the *Financial Times'* "Undercover Economist," wrote a survival guide for multitasking. In it, he asks whether modern life is killing us with the demand to do too many things at once, or whether this is just the new normal. I love this quote: "There is much to be said for focus. But there is much to be said for copperplate writing, or having a butler. The world has moved on."[39] He cites four practices under the umbrella of managing our work: multitasking, task switching, getting distracted, and managing multiple projects. We do all of these every day. And the conclusion from *Getting Things Done,* by productivity guru David Allen, is: make lists with the next thing you plan to do on any given topic.[40] Pretty simple.

Another view of the overloaded social system comes from Alex Pentland in *Social Physics: How Social Networks Can Make Us Smarter*.[41] He suggests that there are three design criteria for our "hypernetworked" societies: social efficiency, operational efficiency, and resilience. While social and operational efficiency are important, I am most interested in resilience in the context of the "nature" principle.

Pentland describes resilience as the long-term stability of our social systems. He points out that many of these (finance, government, work) "periodically seize up, fall apart, or crash and burn."[42] Seems sensible that we should design new systems that might fail less. What comes out of this are principles of distributed leadership, where organizations are beginning to train everyone in the system. Pentland writes: "When decision making falls to those best situated to make the decision rather than those with the highest rank, the resulting organization is far more robust and resistant to disruption."[43]

Natural systems are powerful. We need to pay attention to them and be humbled by them. The main lesson for designed leadership is the interconnectivity of natural systems—and how that plays out in an organization and its community.

Principle 7: Natural systems and their interconnectivity can guide designed-leadership thoughts and actions.

PRINCIPLE 8: APPLY THE JANE JACOBS TEST

The urban planner Jane Jacobs made her name by identifying particular characteristics that make cities work well, and then translating those characteristics into principles that can be applied elsewhere.

Jacobs identified three main qualities for successful city neighborhoods: clear demarcation between public and private space; eyes on the street—eyes belonging to the natural denizens of the street; and the idea that sidewalks need to be active with people—meaning that buildings need to be programmed to create that activity, with coffee shops, bookshops, hardware stores, and so on.[44] These observations were profound, and her good city-making principles can also be translated and extended into the designed leadership space.

For example, the concept of clearly marking public and private space translates into the principle that, as leaders, we need a clear distinction between our public and private voices—and an even clearer idea of when it is appropriate to use one or the other. Mostly, our public voice is the most persuasive and helpful in finding solutions to leadership challenges. But sometimes, it is important to speak from that voice that quietly acknowledges vulnerability and our inner self.

The active street of Jane Jacobs' ideal neighborhood requires an active edge—defined not by blank walls but with an interface that is engaging and interactive. This translates into a principle that suggests an approach to work and home that includes some creative programming, so the workday isn't divided by a blank wall. You need boundaries, but you can benefit from a fuzzy edge that creates the opportunity for a comfortable crossover—perhaps including times for reflection and engagement with colleagues. This is not just a physical space issue; it is a programming possibility to create an intellectually active workplace.

Jane Jacobs identified four key design principles:

1. *Frequent Opportunities to Turn Corners*: Roads and pedestrian routes should be very connected and intersect often, with short blocks to allow people an abundance of choice and efficiency in how they navigate an urban environment.[45]

2. *Mixing It Up*: Different uses (residential, commercial, institutional) in the same place strengthen the identity of a place and those who live there.[46]

3. *Density and Concentration*: The close proximity of the mixed uses to one another strengthens the economy of place and allows people to travel shorter distances for their daily needs.[47]

4. *Eyes-on-the-Street*: When the built environment is at human scale with active programming (cafes, services) bordering public spaces, people watch one another in their daily activities, creating safe and active urban environments where people will feel welcome.[48]

The following are possible guidelines, or standards, for designed leadership à la Jane Jacobs.

1. Turning Thinking Corners: Thinking our way through problems and opportunities for change requires us to connect dots, choose options, and make multiple sets of decisions. One can imagine a parallel between accessibility in a city—where residents have excellent choices about how they move through streets, alleys, and greenways—and accessibility in the organization, where there are multiple options for conceiving and promoting new ideas and innovations. Designed leadership is about finding different ways to move through a problem or opportunity.

2. Mixing It Up: Different ways of thinking strengthen any approach to problem solving. Be methodologically agnostic; mix it up when you are designing your own process. We have discovered, as we learn about designing successful cities, that separating where we work from where we live, and from where we might play, creates transportation challenges. Similarly, segregating ways of thinking isn't helpful. Design leadership supports a diversity of thinking processes and techniques.

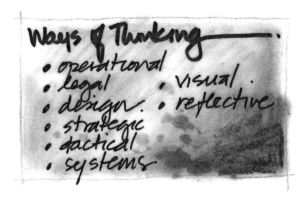

3. Density and Concentration of Ideas: Ideas need to be "dense" in the sense that they piggyback off one another. Even the critics of brainstorming will admit that generating many ideas is better than generating few—if only to exercise our brains. Having a density of ideas on a whiteboard can help us see connections and identify gaps. Designed leadership encourages a density of ideas, approaches, and ways forward.

4. Eyes-on-the-Ball: Eyes-on-the-Street is the classic Jane Jacobs "must do." This translates into the need for leaders to be out on the street (or in corridors and stairways), engaging but mainly observing—with their eyes on the ball. Our observational skills in designed leadership are key. What we

notice in our teams, in our colleagues, and in our daily life can help identify issues before they become problems.

Essentially, the Jane Jacobs test suggests that we follow the four guidelines, incorporating interconnected thinking and doing, different ways of thinking and problem solving, ensuring a density of ideas, and placing leaders on the street to see and be seen. Jacobs' test keeps us on our toes and aware.

Principle 8: Active designed leadership meets the Jane Jacobs test: permeable thinking, mixed methodologies, idea density, and eyes on the ball.

PRINCIPLE 9: ATTEND TO PATTERNS

"If patterns exist in our seemingly pattern-less lives—and they do—then the law of harmony insists that the most harmonious of all patterns, circles within circles, will most assert itself."

—DEAN KOONTZ, *DEEPLY ODD: AN ODD THOMAS NOVEL*, 2013.

A Pattern Language, by Christopher Alexander, is one of my favorite books.[49] It is two inches thick and the paper is thin-thin-thin (at least in my 1978 edition). It is well worn because I refer to it all the time. While written for a built-environment designer audience, its wisdom ranges well beyond that narrow focus.

I thought it might be fun and useful to look at a few of Alexander's patterns through a designed-leadership lens, to see if there are principles that are relevant to design and to business.

Alexander Pattern 1. Independent Regions

"Metropolitan regions will not come to balance until each one is small and autonomous enough to be an independent sphere of culture."[50] Alexander says this principle rests on four factors: (1) the nature and limits of human government; (2) equity among regions in a world community; (3) regional planning considerations; and (4) support for the intensity and diversity of human culture.

The first factor echoes an earlier discussion about size and scale, and about the necessity to match the people or places within our purview with appropriate decision-making processes. Alexander believes that communities reach a critical limit at populations between 2 and 10 million; beyond this size, people become remote from government and leadership. Can we make this same argument about the size of a business or enterprise and the capacity of a leader to be effective? Is there an inevitable tipping point in organizations, or does it depend on the nature and culture of that organization and on the leadership model? Regardless, it's a reminder to always think about the implications of size and culture.

The second factor, equity among regions, relates to the need for communication and appropriate scale so you can share challenges, opportunities, and solutions. In Alexander's view, regions have to be large enough to play globally. Maybe it is the same for businesses, depending on where they want to play. If they want to play locally or regionally, perhaps they can be smaller. If they want to play globally, they need to be of a size and scale to manage the complexity of the global marketplace.

The third factor speaks to self-governance: regions must have the capacity to manage their environments and the environment must be manageable in size. Landscapes like watersheds generally don't organize themselves as systems along political boundaries. This point plays out in organizations: it's important to recognize when business operations are spreading across sometimes isolated departments, and it's important to manage for those variables.

Finally, Alexander argues that independent regions are the receptacles of "beautiful and differential languages, cultures, customs, and ways of life of the earth's people, vital to the health of the planet."[51] If there isn't an independent and regional scale, then it is challenging to keep this differentiation or niche. Is this true in organizations? It is certainly a pattern for a leader to keep in mind: how do you retain the beauties of diversity in an organization while keeping everyone heading in more or less the same direction?

Alexander Pattern 10. Magic of the City

"There are few people who do not enjoy the magic of a great city. But urban sprawl takes it away from everyone except the few who are lucky enough, or rich enough, to live close to the largest centres."[52]

 Think about Barcelona, Boston, Dublin, Haifa, Hamburg, Lisbon, Vancouver, and Zapopan. These are the original Leading Cities, a network of select medium-sized cities engaged in fostering city–university–business–research partnerships (see chapter 6,

Designed Leadership Cases). All the cities in this network are great cities, and they share a great many challenges. How businesses relate to their cities and their patterns can change both the city and the business by making both more active, relevant, and "magic."

Alexander Pattern 18. Network of Learning

"In a society which emphasizes teaching, children and students—and adults—become passive and unable to think or act for themselves. Creative, active individuals can only grow up in a society which emphasizes learning instead of teaching."[53] In the seventies and eighties, we saw the development of suburban research parks—places where universities and businesses came together and created knowledge together. "Knowledge hubs are developing inside cities, in the guise of science or technology parks, creative and design districts, etc. Oftentimes worn-out industrial sites and districts are being regenerated through such hubs or 'creative factories.'"[54]

There has also been a rise of "coworking spaces," like Rocketspace in San Francisco and Reto Zapopan in Mexico. It's a hot trend in an era where technology is redefining work and the workplace, eliminating the need to work in a set place at a set time. According to *Deskmag*, over 110,000 people currently work in one of the nearly 2,500 coworking spaces globally—a number that is growing by 83 percent annually.[55]

Today, Alexander's preference for learning over teaching has serious support in the academic world. It triggers a reference to Ivan Illich and the De-Schooling Society, followed up by an Alexander recommendation: "Instead of the lock-step of compulsory school in a fixed place, work in piecemeal ways to decentralize the process of learning and enrich it through contact with many places and people all over the city."[56]

This points to multisectoral leadership—lifting the practice of learning from the academy and spreading it to other sectors. It points to the city as the classroom—why not learn at City Hall? Why can't grade 9 students learn *in situ* in a business—especially if they can't see the relevance of school and want to quit?

The pattern principle is double-edged: we need to observe and recognize patterns, seeing the world in a way that produces new insights, and we need to remember that patterns sometimes need to be rejigged, reinvented, and redesigned to be useful in the pursuit of designed leadership.

Principle 9: Attend to patterns—recognize them when useful, redesign them if necessary.

PRINCIPLE 10: NEVER FINISHED BUT ALWAYS COMPLETE

"A good solution applied with vigor now is better than a perfect solution applied ten minutes later."

—GENERAL GEORGE S. PATTON, JR., "LETTER OF INSTRUCTION NO. 2," APRIL 3, 1944

Picking up on Patton's theme, in designed leadership we are never finished, but we want to have a sense of completeness, or at least a semicolon on our efforts, always leaving open the possibility for change and evolution. If you wait for something to be ready, or perfectly conceived, you'll get stalled. But if you stop revising just because you've started building, you will waste important opportunities to get to the best result.

The point of the Patton quote is to say, "Get on with it." There are places, times, and states during which a transitory space may be perfect, even if part of that perfection is the expectation that it will be swept away before sundown.

There are facets to the idea of "never finished but always complete." The first is pragmatic: projects need to be on time and on budget. This means that there has to be a rigor and discipline to the strategic design method as it informs designed leadership. Design is not about being sloppy around deadlines and budgets. In fact, there is a huge value to thinking precisely about what needs to be precise—thus leaving room in our minds for the free-flowing type of thinking that is also necessary.

A second facet is that projects are never truly finished; they are dynamic and in constant flux due to internal and external factors. But something that is never finished *can* feel like a problem—more like procrastination and putting things off that really need closure. Projects, programs, ideas, and initiatives need to be executed, but the door should always be open to adding, adjusting, and allowing them to be dynamic.

Organizational change processes suffer from the "this is never going to end" syndrome. My personal example comes from the transformation of a university faculty—the then-faculty of Agricultural Sciences.

It first occurred to me that I could be a different kind of leader when I received a call suggesting that I put my hat in the ring for a deanship. I started thinking about the fact that I was working hard as a director, and that I could perhaps work as hard as dean and be more effective at changing the world.

As director of the Landscape Architecture Program, I was in the world of designers. We all spoke the same language and therefore it seemed like no big deal to operate like designers—to be visual, to have an explicit thinking process, and to collaborate. Not that it was easy, but because of our education and experience, we knew instinctively that design and design processes were effective ways to go about our business.

In the faculty, I was in the world of scientists of all stripes. Theirs was not the world of design (at least as they understood it); it was the world of analysis and experimentation within the narrow focus of their particular discipline. They were generally not accustomed to collaboration, not really into asking broad contextual questions, and they were conservative in their view of what changes might be possible to the faculty and to their lives. I found I had to reset my own approach to leadership. On reflection, I realized that I was using the Jane Jacobs test and many of the other designed leadership principles.

The then-faculty of Agricultural Sciences (now the faculty of Land and Food Systems) was gifted with the infamous "burning platform" that business books talk about as one of the key ingredients for bringing about organizational change. Students were being accepted into the faculty with low averages—which made difficult work for the faculty members. Faculty members included star researchers and star teachers. At the time (1997), the agricultural community itself, for the most part, had little use for research and didn't really appreciate any value-add coming out of the faculty.

The opportunity was ripe for change. A new president, Dr. Martha Piper, had just taken the reins of the University of British Columbia (UBC), and change was in the air. Her strategic plan, named *TREK 2000*, laid out the path.[57]

We needed a design process to transform and reinvent the faculty. We had to codesign a process with the faculty community that was time-limited and would have the capacity to ignite the imaginations and the interest of the students, staff, and faculty members, as well as the community.

Various spaghetti diagrams got me thinking about multiple scenarios for the future. It started as a list, but somehow that was not good enough. Then I recast it as a Venn diagram, which was still inadequate. Only when I added the spaghetti did the whole thing start to take shape. Only then did my own understanding emerge, and I was able to communicate to others.

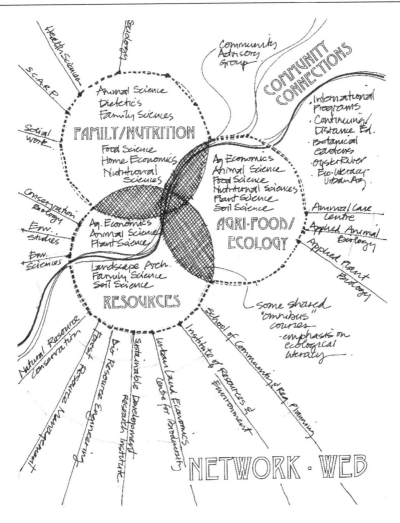

It presented visually the way that the existing faculty interests intersected—
and more important, how they connected to the rest of UBC and beyond. The
diagram then evolved over time, and was refined during the challenge of
finding a new name for the faculty. The faculty name was finally decided
upon and approved by the university some eight years after the transformation process began.

(CONTINUED NEXT PAGE)

[CONTINUED FROM PREVIOUS PAGE]

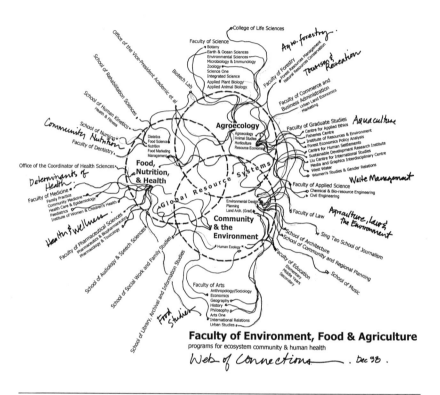

Faculty of Environment, Food & Agriculture
programs for ecosystem community & human health

Web of Connections ——— . *Dec 98* .

There was clearly the need for change. However, the community of potential change agents understandably didn't want any more navel gazing. In response, as dean, I offered up a time-limited process for engaging in a conversation about what we might become as a faculty. I was clear that: (a) there is a clear process; (b) we will start the process in September, and engage it fully until December; and (c) if we don't come to consensus, the process itself will end and I will decide. Fortunately, point (c) did not occur. But it was very helpful for the process to be time-determined and for the community to know that whatever happened, a decision would be made in December, and that particular process would be *complete*—even if the transformation was not *finished*.

The third facet of this idea of finishing and completion involves the concept of managing ambiguity and contradictions. One of the reasons people don't finish is that they feel they have not found the one *right* answer. We tend to prefer to have an answer. That is comfortable. It is hard to get comfortable when you're not sure. But the kinds of problems and opportunities that we now face in business and society rarely fit into a neat package—they are complex and slippery.

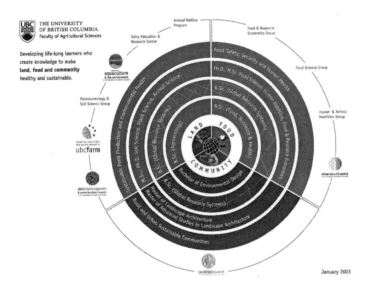

During my time as dean I found lots of contradictions. By embracing them and trying to understand them, and by seeking collaborative solutions, the contradictions become part of the richness of our collective solutions. There were contradictions between expectations of faculty and staff—and conventional wisdom around organizational change, providing rich fodder for implementing and refreshing our workplace.

Therefore, designed leadership is very much about being comfortable with ambiguity and managing the presence of contradictions.

Principle 10: Designed leadership is never finished but always complete and ready to be rethought, reinvented, and redesigned.

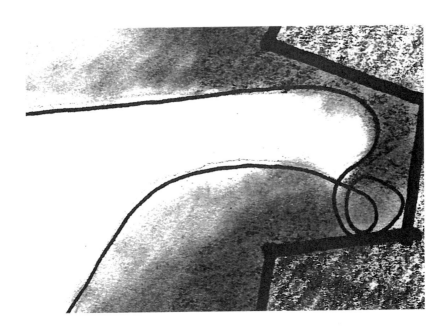

2

Strategic Design Method

Ask, Try, Do

"The definition of design and its role in the world continues to evolve. Broadly speaking, conventional definitions of design revolved around shaping objects and symbols, but more and more design is also expanding into shaping decisions; the latter is how we define strategic design."

—HELSINKI DESIGN LAB TEAM, *IN STUDIO: RECIPES FOR SYSTEMIC CHANGE*, 2011

STRATEGIC DESIGN IS A problem-solving, opportunity-seeking, decision-making process. It is participatory and emergent, rooted in user research. At their best, multidisciplinary teams blend creative and critical thinking techniques to cocreate, test, and launch resilient solutions to big picture or systemic challenges. As noted in the epigraph, strategic design is about shaping decisions.

As a naturally integrative process, strategic design works well in today's complex business environment, especially on prob- 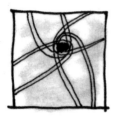 lems that are ill-defined and owned by many. The strategic design method articulated at The University of British Columbia Sauder d.studio[1] is particularly effective for creating both opportunities and clarity when the way forward is not obvious or when our thinking is simply stuck.[2]

Strategic design differs from many other approaches, as it applies cocreative principles that involve all stakeholders in solving problems, leading to innovative and often unexpected solutions.[3]

As a discipline, design has historically been used to produce tangible things—products or services. Strategic design draws on established methodologies from traditional design practices and combines them with creative and analytical approaches from other disciplines, including commerce. The result is a user-driven process that turns inquiry to action.

Some Background

Many people believe that design thinking is a recent phenomenon because it is included on the latest "hot topics" lists. Note the September 2015 issue of the *Harvard Business Review*, in which various luminaries discuss the pros and cons of using design thinking in business. However, the use of the term can be traced to authors such as Peter Rowe, who in 1987 published the first edition of his seminal work, *Design Thinking*—although the book focused on built-environment design.[4] Writing about design methods and processes began even earlier with a variety of authors who explored design from a multitude of angles.[5]

In 1992, Richard Buchanan's influential paper, "Wicked Problems in Design Thinking," brought design solutions to the mainstream, introducing a new audience to design thinking.[6] Until then, design thinking had remained almost exclusively in the design community, where solutions were built, produced, or profiled with an approach that had never been fully adapted for problem solving in the broader community. In 2009, design thinking was brought to a wider audience again, through Tim Brown's TED Talks and his prolific writings.[7]

In my quarter century of applied and academic experience, I have found that using a design approach to problem solving can produce synergy and multiple solutions. Multidisciplinary project teams, while not always easy to manage, can learn to collaborate using their critical and creative capacities, combining data and analysis with open and generative discussion. They can cocreate, test, and launch solutions to big-picture—and often complex—problems.[8] These parameters form the core of strategic design.[9]

My colleagues and I use the term "strategic design" because design is active. It's a verb. Design is not just about thinking, but

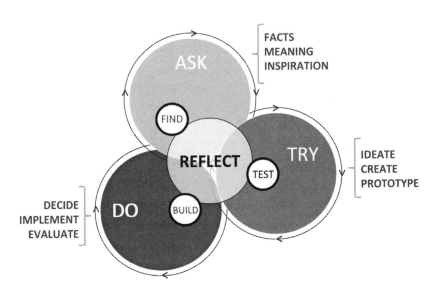

STRATEGIC DESIGN PROCESS CREATED BY MOURA QUAYLE AND ANGELE BEAUSOLEIL©2015

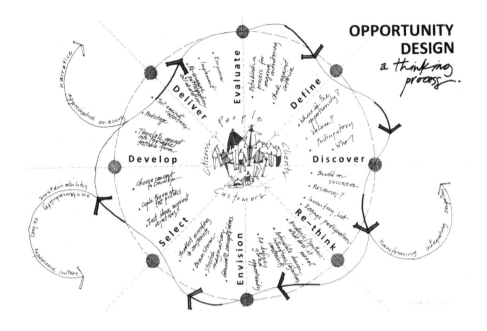

about constantly trying and doing. Sustainable solutions do not stand still, particularly in business. Strategic design utilizes design-thinking techniques, but is a broader term for capturing the art and science of strategic decision making.

ASK

Some call it research. Others call it discovery. Still more call it just plain asking good questions. ASK is a simple word that implies important actions in design and leadership. What are the good questions to ask? When do you ask them? How do you record the answers? How do you unpack the assumptions and reveal the values? You will have lots of questions and sometimes very few answers until you TRY.

TRY

Some call it testing. Others call it prototyping. Still more call it just plain trying out ideas, creating experiments and learning from them. There is an important bridge between ASK and TRY: a bridge from what is to what could be—from current state to future state. The bridge often entails revisions of our  criteria for successful solutions and a revisiting of the problem definition. TRY is where we generate ideas and try them out, test them, refine them, and test them again.

Do

Some call it getting stuff done. Others call it implementing. Still more call it making things happen, and then monitoring, evaluating, and making it happen again. Reflection and iteration are a big part of the process.

ASK

"It is easier to judge the mind of a man by his questions rather than his answers."

—PIERRE-MARC GASTON, *MAXIMES ET RÉFLEXIONS SUR DIFFÉRENTS SUJETS DE MORALE ET DE POLITIQUE*, 1808

"I keep six honest serving men.
(They taught me all I knew);
Their names are WHAT and WHY and WHEN
And HOW and WHERE and WHO."

—RUDYARD KIPLING, *JUST SO STORIES*, 1902

Before formulating the problem in the strategic design method, it is important to think about thinking itself.

In *The Care and Feeding of Ideas*, James L. Adams talks about a problem-solving process that involves identifying our move from Unconscious Incompetence to Unconscious Competence.[10] He uses the example of learning to tie shoes. Look at the chart, and follow along.

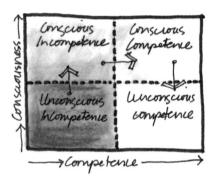

There is a time in life when we don't know how to tie our shoes but are unconscious of our incompetence. We later become aware that we do not know how to tie our shoes; we are conscious and incompetent, and we get frustrated waiting for someone to tie our shoes. Eventually, we learn to tie them ourselves, becoming conscious and competent. Finally, tying shoes becomes a habit, and we are competent and unconscious: we tie our shoes without thinking about it.

So, moving counterclockwise around the chart is a way of describing a learning process. Learning requires that we move

from the lower left corner to the upper left— we become conscious of what we do not know. Moving from the upper left to the upper right and then the lower right is familiar to us— classes, training, lessons. We generally find this fun, especially if we are good at learning. However, we often end up back in unconscious territory.

Living in the lower right is rewarding if we are blessed with good problem-solving habits. But in order to increase creativity, we must be able to move ourselves back to "knowing we don't know" in order to begin the cycle again. We must move from habit to an awareness of our not knowing. Sometimes, this means we need to augment the unconscious with the conscious.

Yet we tend not to be as concerned with unconscious thinking as we should be. After all, humans point to consciousness as that which separates us from all other animals. Consciousness is synonymous with our awareness of experience. Conscious thinking is marvelous—for no other reason than you can think about questions or ideas. We rely on conscious thinking to carry out our lives and to give us free will.

Much of problem solving *is* conscious. While we rely on our unique conscious ability, we are also creatures of habit and programming. To that extent, our problem solving can also be unconscious.

Conscious thinking is often critical thinking—a key component of business thinking. We now recognize that critical thinking, by its very nature, requires the recognition that all reasoning occurs within points of view and frames of reference, that all reasoning proceeds from goals and objectives and has an informational base, that all data must be interpreted, that interpretation involves concepts, that concepts entail assumptions, and that all basic inferences in thought have implications. We now recognize that each of these dimensions of thinking need to be monitored and that problems can occur in any of them.[11]

There is an obvious alignment between the questions that are the platform for excellent critical thinking, and those that permeate the strategic design method and designed leadership.

We can (and should) question the following:

- Ends and objectives
- The status and wording of questions

- The sources of information and fact
- The method and quality of information collection
- The modes of judgment and reasoning
- The concepts that make that reasoning possible
- The assumptions that underlie concepts in use
- The implications that follow from their use
- The point of view or frame of reference within which reasoning takes place

This is the bottom line for critical thinking.

In 1906, William Graham Sumner, professor of sociology at Yale University, defined the modern idea of critical thinking:

> [Critical thinking is] the examination and test of propositions of any kind which are offered for acceptance, in order to find out whether they correspond to reality or not. The critical faculty is a product of education and training. It is a mental habit and power. It is a prime condition of human welfare that men and women should be trained in it. It is our only guarantee against delusion, deception, superstition, and misapprehension of ourselves and our earthly circumstances.[12]

Though it was not named as such, critical thinking is noted throughout recorded human history. Prior to the twentieth century, the chief critical thinker was the philosopher, and in the Western tradition, the chief philosopher was Socrates. Though Socrates left no writing of his own, we have come to learn of the now-famous Socratic method through the writings of his student, Plato. Socrates questioned everything—challenging the most basic of assumptions, and deflating spurious claims to knowledge.[13] This philosophical rigor forms the essence of critical thought, and has been applied throughout history by the world's greatest minds, from Aristotle, to Thomas Aquinas (*Summa Theologica*, thirteenth century), Niccolò Machiavelli (*The Prince*, sixteenth century), René Descartes (*Meditations on First Philosophy*, seventeenth century), Francis Bacon (*The Advancement of Learning*, seventeenth century), Thomas Hobbes (*Leviathan*, seventeenth century), John Locke (*An Essay Concerning Human Understanding*, seventeenth century), Adam Smith (*The Wealth of Nations*, eighteenth century), Isaac Newton (*Mathematical Principles of Natural Philosophy*, seventeenth century), Emmanuel Kant (*Critique of Pure Reason*, eighteenth century), and beyond.[14]

The Ask phase of the strategic design method is arguably the most important and the least utilized.

The most relevant symbol is the question mark (?). The history of the question mark is fascinating.[15] Punctuation has its beginnings in Latin religious texts. Readers, mainly monks, needed to know where various parts of sentences began and ended in order to interpret them correctly. And so it was readers and not authors who were punctuation pioneers, inserting guiding marks into text. At the beginning of the seventh century, silent reading became widely used among scholars. Before that, liturgical texts had generally been either read or sung aloud. In the Middle Ages, the question mark looked different than today's (?). It was more like a period followed by a sharp tilde (~). In modern Arabic, the question mark is reversed so that it can be easily read from right to left. The Greeks and Armenians use different symbols to mark interrogative sentences. In Greek, the semicolon (;) is used instead of a question mark. In Spanish, an upside down question mark begins the sentence, so you know it's a question from the start. In Armenian, the symbol is reminiscent of a snail's house—a stand-alone "shell" in the upper part of the text line called a harcakan.

Arabic	؟
Greek	;
Armenian	՞
Spanish	¿?

Words that are commonly associated with ASK are: "DISCOVER," "RESEARCH," "EXPLORE," "SCOPE," "UNPACK," "OBSERVE," "FORM INSIGHTS," and "REFINE."

Children are almost too good at asking questions, often causing adults either to panic because they don't know the answer (why is the sky blue?) or to lose patience responding to yet another, sometimes challenging, question.

The Ask phase of any process is an invitation to be curious, to be open to the unexpected, and to embrace ambiguity. Amanda Lang writes in *Power of Why* that, "very early on, and often unwittingly, we begin to train curiosity out of kids. Think of the messaging: curiosity killed the cat, led Little Red Riding Hood off the straight and narrow path, and didn't work out so well for Pandora, either."[16] As a result, we generally don't spend enough time and energy asking good questions—ones that open us to the unexpected and bring us new information and insight.

The ASK phase can be understood as a variety of steps taken in any order. However, there is a discipline to the process. It is a rigor of a different sort: you intentionally make decisions on the fly about what is the most useful activity to undertake next. Generally, ASK involves the following lines of inquiry:

- Defining the problem or opportunity
- Unpacking assumptions and values
- Observing and discovering people
- Taking inventory of facts, including knowing who cares about this problem
- Interpreting insights
- Reflecting, rethinking, and reformulating the problem or opportunity

A simple example illustrates the ASK process. I'll continue with this same example for both TRY and DO.

You are planning a weekend getaway for yourself and your partner or friend. What is your process?

What is the problem?

First, think about why you need to get away, and from what. You might think you need to get away because you are stressed at work or tired and burned out. But you could also be yearning for a change of pace—just something to shake yourself up. So the opportunity needs to be explored. Designing the experience will be a response to a certain set of conditions. And in terms of defining the goal, what will the weekend away achieve? Who are the other players? You are asking many questions—of yourself and potentially of your partner or friend.

ASK includes defining the problem or opportunity, exploring, questioning your goals and objectives, as well as defining and "unpacking" values and assumptions. Most important, it is a process that clarifies who cares: users, clients, customers, citizens, and stakeholders. Defining the problem is one of the most important and challenging parts of any problem-solving process. If you spend a lot of time quickly assuming that the problem is "X" and then later find out, it is actually "Y," it is a frustrating and often expensive time-waster—hence the

emphasis in the strategic design method on problem definition.

Here are some other examples of using Ask to open things up. Yves Behar, Swiss designer, entrepreneur, and founder of the Fuseproject design firm, was approached by Puma footware and apparel company to design a new product.[17] But instead of designing a new "thing," he focused on Puma's processes and streamlined everything from packaging to ordering, so that the company "shaved a couple of large toes off its carbon footprint." Asking helped him redefine the problem.

What Do You Need to Know?

Very quickly, your analytical side kicks in and you think: What do I know about my options? What are the facts? What are the constraints? Budget? Travel costs? Time? You take note of what you know and what you don't know.

Another example, from *Speculative Everything*,[18] is Jurgen Bey (a Dutch industrial/product designer), who, when asked to address physical infrastructures such as railway systems and expressways, first questioned the psychological aspect of travel.[19] (Is speed always the most important thing? Or are there other aspects to a journey?). Designers like Bey are "using conceptual design to explore social or political issues."[20] For instance, Bey designed a motorized office chair and desk enclosure to point out how much time we spend in cars in traffic jams.

Designers ask questions that push edges and boundaries (Principle 4), opening up the options for different problem definitions and, as a result, different solutions.

List-making is both a logistical tool and a creative activity. Making lists of what you know and what you don't know can be incredibly useful. An executive coach once assigned me a task: make three lists—activities that I like to do, activities I don't like to do, and activities that other people like me to do because I'm good at them (but that I really don't enjoy). This was illuminating for me. Creating inventories helps us to identify what we know and what we don't know.

Humans often confuse facts (objective information) and interpretations (insights). There is a great deal of difference between the hard, cold certainties of what you see and hear—the facts of your observations—and your interpretation of what you see and hear—your insights. Comingling observations and insights result in a lack of clarity. Carefully separating them reveals our knowledge gaps, showing us where we need to seek more evidence.

Discovery happens using a number of research techniques such as observation, ethnography, interviewing users and experts, and focus groups. Or just plain asking someone. Discovery means leaving the relative comfort of the computer and venturing out into the physical landscape where your problem actually lives. In general, the Ask phase is about asking questions and defining the boundaries of the problem or opportunity. It is focused on people. It is about researching the users and their environment. It is about finding out what is working well and what is not. In the words of Nike president and CEO Mark Parker, "Soak in everything around you. Look deeply. Observing is really the fuel to innovating."[21]

Observation is an important activity for fact-finding; it is a learned skill. It's important to practice both observing and record-ing. Often visual recording is the most useful. What are the behav-ioral patterns that you see in the people you are watching? Are the behaviors different for users such as the very young or very old? What insights can you draw from your observations?

It is important to make observation personal, to understand the human side—to get an insider perspective. If it is impossible to observe your target group because of time or location challenges, create some personas or profiles of various users or stakeholders. This can help you practice empathy—understanding the life of another, stepping into their shoes. One way to do this is to collect old magazines or newspapers and pull out images of people, and then construct their "life stories."

List-making, observing, visual recording all assist in your fact-finding mission.

How does everything fit together?

Once you have collected research from experts and experiencers, you can begin to analyze and clarify your findings. It turns out that your close friends had a great experience in a small town that's just a two-hour train trip from your home. Other friends waxed poetic about an urban experience a short flight away. This tidbit of information sits alongside data including timetables, costs, and rankings in local tourism guides.

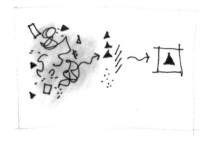

It is easy to undervalue our interpretations or insights as not being factual or irrefutable evidence. David Colander and Roland Kupers reflect on this in their book *Complexity and the Art of Public Policy*:

The problem with scientists structuring frames for policy is that generally they put too little emphasis on intuitive understanding, and too much focus on quantitatively tractable models. For pure science, that's a plus. For policy it can be a problem if the model becomes too firmly rooted in formal modeling, and the scientist using the model does not sufficiently recognize the model's limitations.[22]

Strategic design faces the challenge of balancing the weight of facts with speculation or intuition. Often, moving from facts to insights seeking meaning will trigger even more questions. This means doing more research or checking and verifying your speculations. This is another example of the iterative nature of the strategic design method.

What are the criteria for a successful trip?

You start thinking, "Well, what are my criteria for making this trip a big success? What needs must be met? What factors are mandatory? Budget constraints? Location preferences?" Other criteria may be optional: Would it be nice to have a view, or to have access to good but inexpensive restaurants?

In sum, what criteria will a good solution meet? These criteria come in handy when we evaluate our solutions, so it is a good idea to start noting the critical or mandatory criteria that your solution must meet—as well as the luxuries that are perhaps not critical but would be helpful or useful.

What are the different aspects of the problem?

Finally (and we are now bridging into the TRY part of the process), you can use your insights to unpack the bigger problem into smaller problem /opportunity sets. Starting with "How might we?," you can ask yourself myriad questions: How might we maximize our experience by using a transportation mode we don't usually use?[23] How might we have an adventure in the forty-eight hours we are away?

There are many design methodologies that use different terms for this part of the process. For example, *ExperienceInnovation*[TM], a computer simulation/game created by a partnership between IDEO and Experience Point, calls this phase Inspiration, with the phase's components labeled "Define the Challenge," "Observe People," and "Form Insights."[24] The d.studio team labels components of the ASK phase "Finding Facts," "Finding Meaning," and "Finding Opportunities."[25] The UK Design Council calls the whole process the "Double Diamond" and labels the ASK phase components "Define" and "Discover."[26]

The ASK process is never finished. Reflecting, rethinking, and reformulating problems and opportunities are constant activities of designed leadership.

We often feel deep frustration when we ask questions and don't find answers before we start a process. Frequently, for example, research proposals or requests for work plans demand outcomes up front. We have it backward: it is the process itself that will determine the outcomes. We need to allow the process to unfold to reach the best possible solution. We need to trust ASK.

In summary, the ASK part of ASK, TRY, Do is about exploration and discovery. It's the research piece of the process. And it happens throughout the strategic design method—you will return to ASK frequently as you evaluate your problem definition and find new

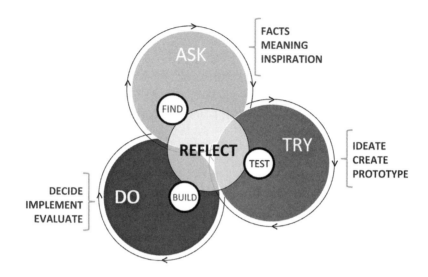

STRATEGIC DESIGN PROCESS CREATED BY MOURA QUAYLE AND ANGELE BEAUSOLEIL©2015

questions that need answers. Here are some of the techniques that can be used in Ask:

- Using Ask words such as "unpack," "observe," "form insights"
- Using questioning words such as "why," "what," "when," "how," "who," "where"
- List-making: inventorying what we know and what we don't know
- Observation, ethnography (understanding how people behave in their cultures), interviews, focus groups
- Visual recording: making visual notes, recording observations and patterns
- Practicing empathy: understanding the lives of others
- Developing criteria, both mandatory and desired. What is a successful solution?

Ask is about finding facts, finding meaning, and finding opportunities.

TRY

"Do one thing every day that scares you."

—ATTRIBUTED TO ELEANOR ROOSEVELT (1884–1962), AND A FEW OTHERS![27]

"Prototyping is a currency for creative dialogue. It embraces play behaviors as a critical component of imagination and ideation."

—IDRIS MOOTEE, CEO IDEA COUTURE,
DESIGN THINKING FOR STRATEGIC INNOVATION, 2013

The TRY phase of the strategic design method is arguably the most fun. It is when you can respectfully silence your adept critical voice and welcome your sometimes-out-of-practice creative voice. The following are activities you can use in the TRY phase:

- Framing manageable questions/problems/opportunities
- Developing evaluation criteria
- Generating ideas
- Choosing ideas to test and prototype
- Checking your criteria further
- (Sometimes) going back to ASK, to redefine the problem
- Landing on a solution

Words that are also commonly associated with TRY are "GENERATE," "CHOOSE," "TEST," "FILTER," "ELIMINATE," "BUILD," "ENVISION," "IDEATE," and "PROTOTYPE."

The TRY phase of the strategic design method is an invitation to take risks and to test ideas. It's about trying things on for size, generating ideas, sorting them, referring back to evaluation criteria, and then getting ready to test again. TRY is iterative.

There is no clean break between ASK and TRY. Rather, the creative process demands a bit of a leap—a change of perspective and tactic, from the past and present (research and analysis) to the future (potential to generate new ideas). Between ASK and TRY lies a crucial transformation task—reframing "problem/opportunity" scope and complexity into smaller, more manageable solution opportunities.

We are now breaking what could be a complex and hard-to-grasp problem into manageable bits. We are refraining from moving too quickly to a solution. Most of us are used to being rewarded for correct answers, so we like to drive to solution. This part of the strategic design method teaches and rewards patience, allowing us to explore the problem or opportunity before we try to find specific solutions.

We are on a quest—we are seeking to find and tackle manageable problems that are part of our bigger problem. Identifying and exploring them helps us find a solution to the bigger challenge. We recognize more clearly the need to unpack the problem—to make it more manageable and bite-sized.

This is a good time to also revisit our mandatory and desirable criteria—the must-haves, and the should-haves or the nice-to-haves. Check in to see if they need revision.

It's time for utilizing the question that I mentioned in ASK: "How might we?"[28]

These are statements that help us move from the present to the future, from the problem to the solution. We want to generate as many "how might we's" as possible to break down a problem. We do this to encourage more exploration and discovery. In other words, we may cycle back to ASK. If the big problem is something like developing a business model for a new company, then a "how might we" could be, "How might we explore the customer needs for the company?" This is a question that you can actually answer.

The TRY part of the ASK, TRY, DO process is about taking the results of your "How might we" questions—and generating some ideas that answer these more manageable questions.

I like the concept of breeding ideas in captivity. I think it came from Professor Ron Kellett in the School of Architecture and Landscape Architecture at The University of British Columbia (UBC).[29] Ron and I taught the first business studio class at the Sauder School of Business. Probably the best-known idea generation technique is brainstorming. Though subject to criticism, brainstorming is useful if you keep in mind its strengths and weaknesses. Brainstorming gives us permission (at least temporarily) to think differently and creatively about a problem or opportunity, deliberately setting aside the many factors that shape and constrain everyday thinking.

In brainstorming, generating ideas is about quantity and quality, but quantity comes first. The founding principle is that one reliable path to a good idea is to generate a lot of ideas. Seemingly impractical, improbable, and even unreasonable ideas are the seeds of the very practical, relevant, and completely reasonable ideas that we seek. The challenge is that we may need a hundred bad ideas to find two or three good ones, but even bad ideas are good fodder for the TRY process. Allow plenty of time to develop the ideas for quality—or to evaluate them as useful or not.

There are a host of idea-generation techniques. You can find a variety on the d.studio website (http://dstudio.ubc.ca) in a section called Techniques Toolkit. Some of my favorite techniques include Freewriting, Story Share, and Six Thinking Hats.

But let's return to the weekend getaway planning, a relatively simple problem that can illuminate how we utilize Try in the process.

How Might We Have at Least One Adventure in the Forty-eight Hours We Are Away?

How might we have an adventure in forty-eight hours? Idea generation techniques help us think up lots of ideas, such as skydiving, windsurfing, spelunking, taking a nighttime walk, not booking anything, or taking potluck. These are all examples of adventure ideas.

Once you have a list of ideas, the next phase requires using your critical capacity to sort them—but how? Again, Kellett comes to the rescue with sift, sort, and rank. These are the activities that can help you select ideas. Remember to revisit mandatory and desirable criteria. Refine them. Use them.

- Efficacy criteria: potential for progress toward solving the problem

- User criteria: potential to fit with the needs and wants of users
- Implementation criteria: potential to initiate, scale
- Economic criteria: potential benefit exceeds potential cost
- Innovation criteria: potential to be a game changer

Sifting involves sifting through and sifting out. Sifting through is putting your ideas through a sieve to isolate which are the most important or useful. Sifting out is separating something, especially something to be discarded, from something else.

Sorting is about separating ideas in terms of their type or class. Sorting means that we come up with idea groupings or themes. You can move ideas around, clump them, cluster them, and easily change your mind.

Ranking is probably a more familiar activity for all of us. We give someone or something a rank or place in an order of preference. Once you have done some sifting and sorting, you can use a matrix to rank your ideas and then decide which ones you want to test or prototype. List your criteria on one axis and your ideas on the other—and use a system to rank them. It can be numerical or lexical—one to ten; good, better, best; poor, fair, good, excellent.

Once you have selected an idea to explore more fully, you will be testing and prototyping as a generative activity. This can happen before, during, and after sifting, sorting, and ranking.

This is a good time to again reflect. Step back. Go up in scale. Look at the context. This part of the process is about testing your ideas and making them better, or eliminating them. It is about failing fast and often. Just remember, this process isn't linear; rather it is cyclical and iterative. The various steps in the strategic design method are like sign-posts which can be utilized or ignored, depending on your tolerance for ambiguity and risk around making an unproductive move.

Choose an idea to work with

Let's work with the idea that "taking a nighttime walk" ranked the highest in our matrix.

It's time to understand this idea more deeply. To this end, prototyping can be generative, as it is just testing your ideas. It is easy to imagine prototyping physical things (objects), but it is harder to prototype concepts, processes, and services.

Prototypes help test assumptions and offer a tool to engage stakeholders. It's important to remember that first attempts rarely succeed. Micro-failures generate learning and move ideas forward quickly.

Here are some examples of ways to prototype:

- Sketching a diagram or flowchart is quick and easy.
- Making a three-dimensional model forces you to think in multiple dimensions.
- Roleplaying and performing skits helps you really get into the process.
- Experimenting with mind-map apps gives you a structure for your prototyping process.

Conceptual Model   Mind Map   Story Board.

- Testing ideas with storyboards is a fabulous way to get deeper into a process.

Ideally, you test your prototypes on other people who ask good questions and make you think about them in a different way.

Prototyping can go on and on. At some point, you must stop and revisit your process: are you still on track with the problem you are attempting to solve or the opportunity you're trying to create? Do your criteria still make sense? This is where reflection and iterating the steps come into play. You can refine and enhance your prototype again and again, based on feedback from experimentation (i.e., going on a nighttime walk), and if you discover the idea won't work, you scrap it (after deriving what you have learned about it), go back to your idea list, and try another one, or go back even further and reframe the opportunity.

The *ExperienceInnovation*™ simulation labels the TRY phase "Ideate" and includes steps called "Frame Opportunities" and "Brainstorm Ideas."[30] I generally label the TRY phase components as "Prototype," "Test," "Refine." The UK Design Council's "Double Diamond" calls the TRY phase "Develop."[31]

TRY never really ends—but at some point you must move on to Do.

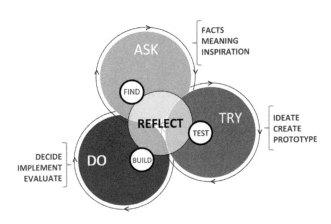

STRATEGIC DESIGN PROCESS CREATED BY MOURA QUAYLE AND ANGELE BEAUSOLEIL©2015

In summary, the TRY part of ASK, TRY, DO is about experimentation and testing. It's the generative piece of the process. And it can happen throughout the strategic design method—you will return to TRY frequently as you evaluate your problem definition and find new ideas or solutions that need to be tested. Here are some of the techniques that can be used in TRY:

- Use ASK words such as "generate," "test," "prototype," and "choose."
- Revisit your mandatory and desirable criteria and refine them.
- Use "How might we" questions to break the problem into smaller pieces.
- Brainstorm and think with your creative voice, silencing your critical voice.
- Use list-making again—this time to generate a quantity of ideas.
- Sort, sift, and rank your ideas to decide what to test or prototype.
- Reflect frequently—step back and away from your activities.
- Design experiments that are cheap and quick.
- Prototype ideas and get feedback—ideally from users.

TRY is about experimenting, prototyping, testing, and refining.

DO

"Remember, to learn and not to do is really not to learn. To know and not to do is really not to know."

—STEPHEN R. COVEY, *THE 7 HABITS OF HIGHLY EFFECTIVE PEOPLE*, 1989

In some ways, Do is the most important part of the strategic design method. If we never get to Do, what is the point?

In 1963, Ted Levitt, a former editor of the *Harvard Business Review*, wrote a piece on innovation titled "Creativity Is Not Enough," which said:

> Those who extol the liberating virtues of corporate creativity over the somnambulistic vices of corporate conformity may actually be giving advice that in the end will reduce the creative animation of business. This is because they tend to confuse the getting of ideas with their implementation—that is, confuse creativity in the abstract with practical innovation; not understand the operating executive's day-to-day problems; and underestimate the intricate complexity of business organizations.[32]

I have sympathy for Levitt's viewpoint. Design is often thought of as that fluffy, creative side of any process, but this could not be further from the truth. The design practitioner is always considering the practical, the analytical, the reality of the situation. Designers have the capacity to venture into creativity—but they should always return to "how can we get this done," "how can we implement," "how can we show results and solutions?" Designed leadership is grounded in Do.

However, I disagree with Levitt as he paints people who show creativity as being less responsible for their actions. Maybe this was the case in 1963. But now, there is a much more creative and implementation-oriented cohort of businesspeople who understand the importance of both creativity (examining a problem from all sides) and implementation.

How we work as teams or as individuals in idea generation or in implementation depends on the culture of our organization, our relationships, our learning styles and the spaces we work in—a pretty complex mix. So I wouldn't discard brainstorming or other idea-generation techniques—they are a part of the process, useful at a point in time, and sometimes very effective.

Do: Implement, Evaluate, Innovate

Other processes label Do as implementation or delivery.

Words that are also commonly associated with Do are "DELIVER," "EVALUATE," "MEASURE," "MAKE," "LAUNCH," and "REVIEW."

Do encompasses several phases; implementation is the first. This means working with the relevant people to develop a plan to roll out your solution, or to conceive of a staged approach to enable ongoing improvement of the outcomes.

In the case of the forty-eight-hour adventure, an implementation plan might include a budget, timeline, and milestones. It is essential to bring all your ideas and solutions together in a coherent plan. Ideally, the budget and timeline discussion will have entered the conversation far earlier in the process, but Do is the time for refinement and final decisions: buying tickets, making reservations, and so on.

Do is often inspiring because it is about creating something tangible.

Another important and often forgotten aspect of Do is to evaluate: Establish a process and metrics for ongoing evaluation. Consider viewing the solution as a beta model, open to continuous improvement.

The forty-eight-hour adventure may end up being a beta model that you use in the future; if so, it's important to have a sense of what worked and what didn't so that you can make improvements.

Another aspect of Do is to innovate: Design an ongoing innovation strategy into your production and quality assurance processes, being sure to include user research in your strategy.

The development of creative ideas does not necessarily imply their implementation. A recent study examined the relationship between creativity and implementation, exploring the possibility that this relationship is "regulated by individuals' motivation to put their ideas into practice and [by their] ability to network, or, alternatively, [by] the number of strong relationships they maintain."[33] Being successful at Do often means developing a supportive network or

What have you learned?

In the case of the forty-eight-hour adventure, what kind of disruptive innovation could you build into the next experience, given what you've learned?

developing a sense of buy-in from the organization: "The findings of this study support this argumentation and suggest that unless actors are motivated to push for the realization of their ideas and skilled at developing strong buy-in relationships, creativity is likely to be lost."[34]

Expanding how designed leadership supports teamwork, collaboration, and production, the final message in this chapter is how I have used the technique of forming small groups of diverse people (circles) to engage a problem in multiple contexts to assist in generating and implementing ideas. As Michael West titles his paper in Applied Psychology: "Ideas Are Ten a Penny: It's Team Implementation Not Idea Generation That Counts."[35] I might not go that far, but there is no doubt that making things happen is important.

Circles

In my own built-environment design work, I often incorporate circular forms. The sitting walls I designed were always circular, encouraging sitting and socializing.

My introduction to the circle as a participatory process was with Vancouver's City Plan process in the early 1990s.[36] Vancouverites were invited to create circles of friends, neighbors, and colleagues to talk and dream about the city. Somehow, the call to "create a circle" sent a more fun and engaging message than "form a group." The engagement in the circle process was key to implementing the strong neighborhoods that Vancouver boasts today because many voices were heard by the city planners, politicians, and the neighbors themselves. Circles encourage a diversity of thought and allow ideas to be explored and improved upon.

LAND AND FOOD SYSTEMS CIRCLES

I used the concept of circles to assist the transformation process of the UBC faculty of Land and Food Systems (formerly Agricultural Sciences) as its dean. Faculty members were blunt with me: "We are tired of navel-gazing sessions with facilitators that take us nowhere. Moura, just make a decision and get on with it."

However, I knew that would not work, so we designed a process with a beginning, a middle, and an end. As I mentioned in chapter 1, Principle 10: Never Finished but Always Complete, processes require a time frame to be effective. To signal the start of the process, we handed out a scenario workbook at the September community meeting of faculty, staff, and students. Everyone was invited to form circles, using the scenario workbook as a guide.

Within a week or so, we had about twenty-five circles, highlighting a significant appetite for engagement through discussion and debate. The circles achieved many objectives: providing input into the action plan, bringing members of the community together (crossing disciplines), and doing some necessary venting within a limited time frame. The circle process helped lead to fairly speedy implementation of the action plan, including de-departmentalization and re-visioning of the future of the faculty, with an eventual rebranding and name change.

BRITISH COLUMBIA MINISTRY OF ADVANCED EDUCATION CIRCLES

Another circle adventure came at the British Columbia Ministry of Advanced Education (AVED), where I had the opportunity to help the ministry evolve from an institutional focus to a more student-centered focus. I was an implant—an academic in a government culture. Again, it was about designing a process: information, ideas, learning, knowledge, understanding, innovation, and leadership. We defined evolution as the incremental and qualitative improvement of the organization. To respond to the challenges and opportunities of the future, the "Evolving AVED" process was designed to produce a plan for the formative five-year period up to 2010.

The circles didn't have as much impact in the ministry as in the faculty, perhaps because I found the circle process difficult to establish and challenging to sustain. I believe the ripple effect of Evolving AVED was that the ministry staff got more engaged and began to think more strategically about their mission and what they *do* on a daily basis.

Circles have turned out to be an interesting engagement tool. They provide lots of opportunity for small-group work in balancing the critical and the creative, embracing ASK, TRY, and DO, while contributing to implementing ideas, practices, and organizational change.

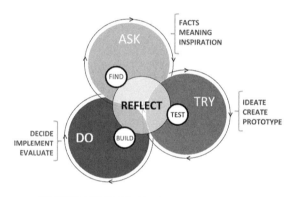

STRATEGIC DESIGN PROCESS CREATED BY MOURA QUAYLE AND ANGELE BEAUSOLEIL©2015

In summary, the DO part of ASK, TRY, DO is about deciding and implementing. It's the tangible action piece of the process. Here are some techniques that can be used in DO:

- Use Do words such as "deliver," "measure," and "review."
- Decide on budget, timeline, and milestones: set deadlines.
- Engage a team and develop clear roles and responsibilities.
- Record your learning about the method and the results.
- Develop a monitoring/evaluation system for continual learning.
- Keep innovating and improving the results.

Do is about choice, implementation, evaluation, and innovation.

PART II

Learning and Practice

THIS SECTION BRINGS TOGETHER the learning and practices of designed leadership based on the principles and methods of the previous section. The learning-practice idea is about rethinking, redesigning, and rebuilding our ways of thinking to help develop a designed leadership skill set.

In 2010, the World Economic Forum theme was "Improve the State of the World: Re-think, Re-design, and Re-build."[1] These positive, active verbs are key to resetting for designed leadership.

Rethinking

In June 2014, Thomas Friedman hosted one of his "Next New World: Work 2.0" conferences.[2] A project of the *New York Times*, the day-long symposium brought together 300 invited guests, including educators, employers, and social entrepreneurs. The day's objective was to explore how quickly our hyperconnected world is changing how we respond with new business models and new ways to help our children learn how to reinvent themselves for optimal success.

Conferences, in general, are becoming more challenging for those of us who fidget in a seat after twenty minutes or who have a short attention span. However, "Work 2.0" and Friedman kept my attention throughout the day. This was partly due to the themes: the technology shifts that are changing our world, the impact on industries and business, the skills required and the implications for K-12 and postsecondary education. As Friedman adroitly put it: the subtext of the day was the question, Where will our kids get jobs?

In many ways, rapid advances in technology threaten commerce as we know it, and as many businesses practice their trade. Rethinking is needed. Andrew McAfee, the cofounder of the MIT Initiative on the Digital Economy, made the point that technology is a complement, not a substitute: jobs are digitally complemented.[3] He also echoed the need for flexibility and adaptability where we no longer expect one job and one career for life. Careers will be spent as thinkers not as workers. People-to-people services will be key. We need boundary spanners—people with the skills to translate and convert ideas into action.

Rethinking for designed leadership is not just about responding to technological advances. It is

Ways of Knowing:[5]

- Sense perception,
- Memory,
- Reason,
- Language,
- Emotion,
- Faith,
- Imagination,
- Intuition.

about exploring our various "ways of knowing," otherwise known as the theory of knowledge. Eileen Dombrowski and her colleagues[4] have created an important curriculum for International Baccalaureate students that identifies eight ways of knowing. These provide a framework for thinking critically about subjectivity, objectivity, fallacies in our reasoning, and evaluating knowledge claims—so important now in the age of the Internet. These ways of knowing also provide an added framework for the strategic design method.

Redesigning

Part of engaging in designed leadership is being open to personal reinvention—redesigning what you do and how you do it. A special 2009 issue of the *Harvard Business Review* on "Leadership in the New World" featured an article about the different modes of leadership  that are required in this new world: "Leadership in a (Permanent) Crisis," by Ronald Heifetz, Alexander Grashow, and Marty Linsky.[6] They write: "Leadership is an improvisational and experimental art," which often requires new leadership practices. These new practices require a palette of adaptation techniques, and some of these come from the designed leadership tool kit. Heifetz, Grashow, and Linsky discuss the need to foster adaptation (the idea of "next" practices), embrace disequilibrium (keep people on their toes, but not too much), and generate leadership (give people at all levels in any organization the opportunity to lead experiments).[7]

I am intrigued with the idea of rethinking business back toward commerce. We have lost the use of this great word, which has a much broader, and (to me) more useful, meaning in terms of rethinking leadership.

Commerce is the whole system of an economy that constitutes an environment for business. The system includes legal, economic,

I have crossed lines, changed sectors, and made moves from business to academia, academia to government, and then back to academia (with a business focus). When people change sectors, it illuminates the issue of knowledge sharing and transfer in often disparate knowledge cultures. Such a change causes a redesigning or reinvention of how we act as leaders.

When I moved from being a dean to being a deputy minister, I was leaving behind the relatively nonhierarchical culture of the academy for government, characterized by more hierarchy but also by clearer, and often faster, decision making. As an outsider, a noncareer public servant, I brought a perspective that could shed light on processes and programs in a way that insiders could not. That said, the government culture was hard to nudge along with new processes or ideas.

An outsider perspective can often reveal the lack of knowledge integration from other domains. These knowledge gaps are emphasized, for example, when people from different disciplines or sectors get in a room together. Public servants wonder why academics cannot provide easy-to-access research in order to help develop evidence-based policy. Citizens wonder how their investment in academic research improves the quality of their lives. Businesspeople wonder about the regulatory environment that sometimes fails to set up businesses for sustainable success. Academics wonder why their institutions do not reward them for research and action that is applied, relevant, and accessible.

Fresh eyes are helpful in solving deeply embedded systemic issues. Fresh eyes can shake things up. Practicing designed leadership means bringing fresh eyes to as many situations as you can to move to a resilient reset of organizations.

political, social, cultural, and technological systems that are in operation in any country. Thus, commerce is a system or an environment that affects the business prospect of an economy or a nation-state.[8]

Commerce, and understanding our economy as part of our environment, is now a critical key to the health, sustainability, and resilience of our planet. The more quickly we recognize the idea of commerce as an important system that requires integration with other systems, the better. Concepts such as clusters, hubs, planning principles, and business principles form more bridges between business and design that need to be recognized or celebrated.

Rebuilding

Rebuilding begins with education. Return-ing to the example of the *New York Times* Work 2.0 symposium, host Friedman also interviewed Laszlo Bock, former (2006–2016) senior vice-president of People Operations at Google. This interview informed Friedman's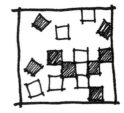
insightful column on "How to Get a Job at Google."[9] During the symposium interview, Friedman asked Bock what Google is looking for in employees. I was very interested in the answer from a com-pany that, at the time in 2014, received 11,000 applications a day and held a workforce of which 14 percent had no college degrees. Bock described four qualities: general cognitive ability—the ability to learn and keep learning; emergent leadership—people willing to step in when there is a problem and step back when they are not needed; cultural fit—comfort with ambiguity, humility; and expertise in technology roles, but with what he called a portfolio approach.

This list sounded to me like a great one for business schools, and for postsecondary education generally. These traits align with the strategic-design mindset: being open to learning, listening (not talking), being comfortable with ambiguity, and being T-shaped—meaning that they exhibit general breadth (the horizontal bar of the "T"), underpinned by significant expertise/depth in some area (the vertical bar of the "T").

Rebuilding also requires disruptions. Forces that continue to change and shift commerce are often the result of what the McKinsey Global Institute describes as disruptive technologies.[10] In a 2013 report, the McKinsey team looked at technologies through a series of lenses, asking throughout: Is the technology advancing rapidly or experiencing breakthroughs? Is the potential scope of the impact broad? Will significant economic value be affected? Will economic impact be potentially disruptive by 2025?

The ideas of reset, rethink, redesign, and rebuild reflect the iterative nature of the work that leaders do.

Designed leadership is about tapping into the mind-set, tools, and techniques of the designer, to help shape more effective leadership. It centers on a reset of the person, of ways of being (mindset), and of ways of engaging one another (relationships and communication style).

This set of chapters tackles ways to think about resetting for designed leadership.

Seeing is understanding. To imagine is to exist. "Thinking Visually and Spatially" (chapter 3) reviews systems of visual and spatial literacy to reveal why and how we can all benefit from improved visual thinking skills. Active vision, our current understanding of human perception, and visual queries illuminate the importance of thinking visually. Practicing visual and spatial thinking is the groundwork for designed leadership.

"Places to Practice Designed Leadership" (chapter 4) describes spaces of collaboration and creativity—studios and other nurturing environments. There are a host of places in which to practice designed leadership, and there are some places and environments that are more conducive than others. Our environment and our context can help us make the best possible decisions, generate the most elegant solutions, and develop and live the most inspired and grounded leadership.

"Learning and Education for Designed Leadership" (chapter 5) explores the value that designed leadership brings to the leader as learner, mentor, and teacher. Leaders should act and simultaneously learn—about others and about themselves. And there are a variety of institutions and opportunities for learning about the designed leadership.

While self-awareness, places to practice, and continuous learning are all important, so is the capacity to build relationships and work collaboratively. "Designed Leadership Cases" (chapter 6) refers less to when and how we are creative, and more to the importance of collaboration and the exchange of ideas, voices, and experience when solving wicked problems. Three cases are described: The Campus City Collaborative (City Studio), Leading Cities, and the Pacific Coast Collaborative.

And finally, "Take-Away" (chapter 7) outlines seven key points to ponder about designed leadership.

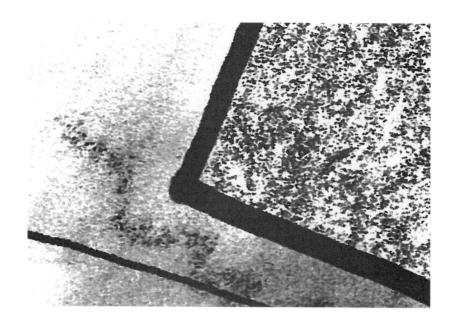

3

Thinking Visually and Spatially

"Drawing is a way of coming upon the connection between things, just like metaphor in poetry reconnects what has become separated."

—JOHN BERGER, INTERVIEW IN *THE SCOTSMAN*, MAY 30, 2011

WHAT IS MY MOST IMPORTANT thinking tool? I would say drawing and visualization—seeing what could be and using visual tools to reach that future. Colin Ware in *Visual Thinking for Design* writes,

Visual thinking tools are especially important because they harness the visual pattern finding part of the brain. Almost half the brain is devoted to the visual sense, and the visual brain is exquisitely capable of interpreting graphical patterns, even scribbles, in many different ways. Often, to see a pattern is to understand the solution to a problem.[11]

Truly seeing is understanding. To imagine is to exist and to seek meaning. In that context, this chapter draws attention to the visual as a signal for how we should work, taking full advantage of building our capacity to think visually and spatially. The concept of the visual-spatial thinker illuminates systems of visual and spatial literacy to reveal why all of us need visual thinking skills.

We view the world through different-colored lenses and different lens strengths. We can use a microscope or a telescope, depending on how we want to see. We can shield our view with dark glasses or clarify it with contact lenses.

The optic nerve is key to seeing. And another definition of nerve is what is sometimes required to tackle challenges. It takes courage to live with ambiguity, to not have *right* answers (often), and to be willing to ask tough questions that frequently don't have any answers at all. Colin Ware writes:

> Meaning is what the brain performs in a dance with the external environment. In this dance tokens of meaning are spun off into electronic and social media and tokens of meaning are likewise picked up. New meaning is constructed when patterns already stored within the brain are combined with patterns constructed from external information.[12]

Starting with the naked eye and moving along to 3-D glasses, humankind has developed many different aids that allow us to see in a multitude of ways. But when we get right down to the complications of seeing, thinking, and doing, do we casually just look, or do we actually *see*?

Considering the sheer volume of information that most problems or opportunities now require to be understood and solved, we require different kinds of "seeing;" visual and spatial lenses can help inform our problem-solving and opportunity-seeking processes.

The Naked Eye

The eyes have it: engineered by Mother Nature, the eye is both receiver and communicator: the bird's-eye view; the eye of the storm; the public eye; the apple of my eye; eye candy; without batting an eye; pull the wool over my eyes; I only have eyes for. . . . Eyes have to be trained to see. Observation is a key platform for discovery. What we observe is then the basis for our insights, our problem definition and our solutions. Whether it is sighting down a pool cue to line up just the right spin, or sighting a problem, we need our naked eye and 100 percent of our attention.

Spectacles, aka Glasses

Some of us need a different kind of help to really see— in a physiological sense. The invention of spectacles profoundly influenced progress in the arts and sciences. Now we have bifocals, contact lenses, progressive lenses—and a myriad of different eyeglass shapes and sizes.

Magnifying Glass

When we really want to play detective and see close up.

Binoculars

The quick and easy way to zoom in and make the background feel like foreground. Especially useful for seeing moving objects like eagles or speeding Vespas.

Telescope

Several disconnected discoveries led to the telescope— whether the legend of the Phoenicians who were BBQ-ing on the sand and discovered glass (c. 5000 B.C.) is true or not, glass comes into the picture long before the telescope, around 2200 B.C. From there it took another 1700 years (~424 B.C.) for Aristophanes to discover that a glass sphere filled with water could start fires. At least another 1800 years passed before we used lenses to study the stars.[13]

Microscope

Like the telescope, the microscope has come to us through a series of breakthroughs over the ages.[14] But where the telescope took us to the cosmos, the microscope led to countless vital findings about the nature of our infinitesimal worlds. In the seventeenth century, Anton van Leeuwenhoek chased his curiosity after viewing images produced from a microscope in Robert Hooke's *Micrographia*. He proceeded to build his own lenses, and soon discovered the living world of microorganisms. He's now considered the father of microbiology.[15]

Kaleidoscope

Invented in the early nineteenth century, the kaleidoscope came about after Sir David Brewster, a Scottish physicist and inventor, undertook a series of experiments on the polarization of light by successive reflections between plates of glass. The name Brewster gave to his invention comes from the Greek words, *kalos* or beautiful, *eidos* or form, and *skopeō*, to see—to see beautiful forms.[16] Perhaps the kaleidoscope is the most useful design tool of all of these visual aids; it is inspirational in its constantly changing colors and patterns, and it can keep us from our habit of looking at everything in the same way.

3-D Glasses

"In the fourth-generation models of 3-D glasses . . . the complicated work is done by the graphics card, and the lightweight LCD glasses flick so rapidly between the two images that all we see is crystal-clear, 3-D images."[17] Lucky us.

Essential Skills: Visual and Spatial Literacy

While many people stop listening when the conversation turns to design, those same people often perk up when they hear the word "innovation." Yet, design and the seeing involved in design processes are a prerequisite for innovation. The critical and creative thinking processes ideally result in innovation—a new or better process, product, way of looking at the world, or way to solve a social challenge like malnutrition or poverty. Innovation. It's the lifeblood of our global economy and a strategic priority for virtually every CEO around the world. A 2011 IBM poll of 1,500 CEOs identified creativity as the number-one indicator of "leadership competency" of the future.[18] In the PWC 2014 CEO Survey, innovation was highlighted as a competitive advantage. When CEOs worry about their future: "The answer is to innovate. More than a third of U.S. CEOs say new products and services now offer the main opportunity for growth for their companies in 2014."[19]

In *The Innovator's DNA*, the authors talk about innovators as consummate questioners who always challenge the status quo. They are intense observers and big-time networkers, constantly sharing insights while searching for new ideas by talking to different people, trying out new experiences, and piloting new ideas.

They also practice five essential skills that are the backbone of strategic design:

1. Associating (making connections)
2. Questioning (inquiring deeply)
3. Observing (people's behavior and life)
4. Idea networking (not resource networking)
5. Experimenting[20]

The strategic design method emphasizes and builds a skill set in these five areas. Then we add the sixth and seventh essential skills: *thinking visually* and *thinking spatially*.

Thinking Visually

What does thinking visually mean? Visual literacy combines two skills: visual acuity and visual expression. Visual acuity is seeing information or diverse messages with clarity and accuracy.[21] People with excellent visual acuity are perfect witnesses to accidents, for example, because they notice and remember the details of what they saw.

Visual expression is about creating or conveying visual messages, such as drawing a clear map for a tourist who is lost. Visual acuity is about receiving messages, and visual expression is about sending them.

When we express ourselves visually, we generally choose from three types of message: representation, abstraction, and symbolism.

Representation is rarely used in everyday visual thinking—it captures what we actually see and experience, as a camera or a representational painting does.

More useful to us, and more common, is abstraction, where we purposely distill meaning in our visual message.

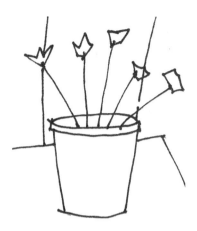

Finally, symbolism works when we use a surrogate or substitute image for what we actually see; we use this symbolic language frequently when we need visual shorthand.

Studies of creative visual thinking reveal common elements among designers, artists, and scientists. Ware, in *Visual Thinking for Design*, identifies the steps as follows:

1. The visual concept is formed inside our heads.
2. A loose scribble externalizes the concept.
3. Scribble is visually critiqued and tested.
4. Original scribble is modified.[22]

The power of sketching as a thinking tool comes from a combination of four things. The first is the fact that a line can represent many things because of the flexible interpretive pattern-finding capacity of the visual system. The second has to do with the way sketches can be done quickly and can be just as easily discarded. Starting over is always an option. The third is the critical cognitive skill of interpreting lines in different ways. Part of this skill is the ability to project new ideas onto a partially completed scribble. The fourth is the ability to imagine new additions to a design.[23]

Visual literacy means becoming familiar with the language of vision and sight, being able to see (and perhaps have insights), and then recording and interpreting this data. Thinking visually is a way to test ideas, to see them in a form that goes beyond words. Diagrams and other visual representations of ideas bring an entirely new means of communication to discussion. Sometimes words can be misconstrued, but clear, concise drawings and diagrams often elicit the kinds of questions that help develop a shared understanding. Simple drawings or sketches can evoke new ideas and questions: What did you mean by this juxtaposition? or What does that line or box signify? or Why did you separate that idea from this idea? Visual representations can play a clarifying role, as well as a creative role, depending on the quality of the representation and the timing of its introduction into the strategic design process. In the business world, visual thinkers have a competitive advantage. They can see the world and diagram its complexity in a way that makes it readable and comprehensible.

Thinking Spatially

Spatial literacy is a type of visual literacy, in that it is about receiving and sending messages in three dimensions. It's important to see the world not as a set of two-dimensional flat planes, but as having a third dimension. Little recognized is the learned ability to recognize patterns as we look to solve problems of a nonspatial nature. As a team engages in building a business, for example, members will  analyze the potential customer base or the market—spatial literacy allows insights necessary to both comprehend and draw insights from that data.

Spatial literacy involves our ability to visualize and interpret. A person who is spatially literate is an avid map reader and the quintessential navigator. We all know about these characteristics. Spatially challenged people find it almost impossible to visualize and interpret any of the kinds of directional and distance relationships that are so fundamental to understanding and solving problems. Most of us have been lost with a spatially challenged colleague (or partner) who had volunteered to navigate our route through a new city. Yet there are similar examples of people who are spatially gifted; we marvel at the soccer player who can clearly judge direction, speed, and acceleration of the ball with unbelievable precision.

The University of Redlands has created a Centre for Spatial Studies that empowers "faculty and students to integrate spatial thinking in their academic, personal, and professional lives."[24] Research projects span the disciplines including projects on mapping civic culture and social capital in the city of Redlands and creating interactive, layered, and detailed maps of individual Holocaust survivor journeys.[25] This is thinking ahead as technologies develop further around Geographic Information Systems (GIS), Global Positioning Systems (GPS), and applications not yet invented or imagined.

Like visual literacy, spatial literacy rejects the isolation that some disciplines manifest, such as mathematics or economics. Like design, these visual languages describe a way of thinking and seeing that crosses disciplines. And as a result, they should be embedded and integrated into our learning processes and experiences.

Visual Messaging: Generative and Open

While a workplace team might speak the same verbal language, our culture, background, and experiences are often no longer common. Visual language can help illuminate the areas where we might verbally miscommunicate. Sometimes the visual can clarify. Other times it can mystify—also an important role in the creative process. We can see patterns and gaps when we make our ideas visual.

Understanding ways of seeing—how we view and *re*-view the world every day—is key in developing visual literacy. Strategic design for transformation in business and politics requires looking at the world through different lenses and with different perspectives. We can imagine viewing the world as background, middle ground, and foreground.

There are innumerable concomitant core values in the understanding of background, middle ground, and foreground. Analyzing a business or a business decision using this visual tool provides us with a new vantage point from which to generate ideas and forward movement. And just as telescopes enable us to see the stars, we can glean great value from a visual discipline that allows us to consider our opportunities and challenges from multiple perspectives. Visual and spatial thinking can help us both realize the complexity of most problems faced in design leadership and find ways to pull apart the problem.[26]

Background is the biggest context and the furthest away. It is often blurry, softened by distance or fog, but sometimes when the light is just right, the background emerges clear and crisp. The background is the critical context. We need help to see and understand the long-term view, but it is also important to provide direction and orientation for immediate decisions.

Middle ground is clear but still not touchable; fine details aren't evident but you can see whitecaps, waves, and small vessels bucking the tide, and binoculars work to bring objects into focus. The middle ground of a problem is often the most challenging—it is neither the context nor the specifics. It is where the fog might be, literally and figuratively.

Foreground is up close and in your face. There is no hiding from the foreground, and to try to ignore it would be folly. Here is where the magnifying glass or microscope is invaluable. For problem seeking, the foreground can offer a wealth of information—whether it's illuminating or overwhelming. Perhaps expectedly, this is where your observational skills come to the fore.

Transformations: Verbal-Visual, Visual-Verbal, Visual-Visual

Design and thinking strategies are about transformation. Built-environment designers move from a written program for a particular space, like a library, to the design of the space and the place: a verbal-visual transformation.

Similarly, when we visit a particular site or landscape, we take in the spirit of the place from visual cues—and then we transform those sensibilities into creating a new space or place: a visual-visual transformation.

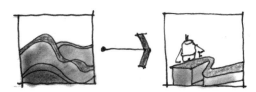

These transformations are common to many design disciplines, but they are also useful for all types of idea generation and creative thinking. They make the familiar strange and the strange familiar. For example, what if you used the image of an orange and the various ways you can manipulate an orange to develop a business plan?

The business plan can be thought of holistically (the whole orange), in discrete parts (the segmented orange), or flattened out (the squished orange). In the process of learning about transformation, you learn at the same time that the whole world around us is an important source of information and inspiration. Transformations are a means of developing greater intimacy with any particular idea and, in the process, expanding one's understanding of the nature and potentials of the idea.[27]

For verbal-visual transformations, our sources are many: dictionaries, metaphors, quotations, book passages, power words, allegories, or poetry. We are looking for images, a sequence of ideas, attitudes, a sense of time, and an overriding intent. We can use words, for example, to get a feel for the function of an object, to have an idea in association with other ideas, or as something that reminds us of other ideas.

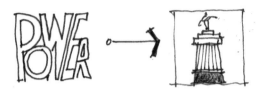

For visual-verbal transformations, our sources include art, photographic images, night skies, geometry, tangled gardens, hardware stores, maps, ballet, and spices. We are looking for moods, colors, textures, humor, empathy, a sense of importance, uses, decay, and meaning. We can use our sources as a literal translation of the nature or sense of the object, as an item with a strong formal structure, as a specific process or way of achieving a result, or as an object that establishes a strong phenomenological response—a response that evokes a powerful experience.

Of course, there are people from Hollywood to Bollywood who perfectly understand the tricks of visual-verbal-visual transformation. The best writers and filmmakers pursue an optimal mix, using text and imagery to convey information in a way that captures the audience's emotion and imagination, not merely their attention.

We are generally entranced by the film experience—so why would we pass up the opportunity for a visually-enhanced business or life in general? Especially when such an opportunity could give us enhanced capacity to make ourselves understood. Why not utilize this neural hotline to creativity?

Transformational techniques help us think visually and think differently. And in the process, they wake up sleeping ideas that we didn't even know we had.

Taking Visual Notes: Drawing as Thinking

One of my favorite professional design books is *Visual Notes for Architects and Designers* by Norman Crowe and Paul Laseau. It is one of those books that I had to re-buy because it was falling apart from overuse. In their introduction, Crowe and Laseau talk about taking visual notes to record a scene or situation instead of using a camera. "Although a camera can be used creatively, it does not require any more than a superficial interaction between the observer and the view. . . . Le Corbusier said that cameras 'get in the way of seeing.'"[28] There is something about the communication between the hand and the eye that causes us to think through, analyze, and code what we are seeing and what we are drawing. This, of course, makes sense if you are notetaking a cityscape, for instance. But I think it is transferable to using visual language for communicating ideas to yourself or a group. There is an important engagement in questioning relationships—between lines, squares, circles, and other forms.

Another example comes from Jonah Lehrer's book *Imagine: How Creativity Works*.[29] He tells a story about the graphic designer, Milton Glaser, who decided to draw a portrait of his mother:

That sketch taught me something interesting about my mind," he says. "We're always looking, but we never really see." He didn't really "see" her until he tried to draw her. "When you draw an object, the mind becomes deeply, intensely, attentive," Glaser says. "And it's that act of attention that allows you to really grasp something, to become fully conscious of it. That's what I learned from my mother's face, that *drawing is really a kind of thinking.*[30]

Just as Edward de Bono invented the Six Thinking Hats to emphasize that we need specific time to think in a set of particular ways, perhaps we need to don spectacles that are special for particular kinds of observation. In addition to thinking caps, we need observing spectacles.

Visual and spatial thinking is the ability to receive diverse inputs and make sense of them for future action. Sometimes the action will be immediate in response to a crisis. Sometimes a vision of the future is required to guide us. Such as vision allows you to have the will to act on what you see and understand, articulate core values clearly, become a visual business thinker, embrace the cycles of learning, boldly create places and spaces for business thinking, record your own narratives about transformation, and share these narratives with the world.

Learn to speak visual.[31]

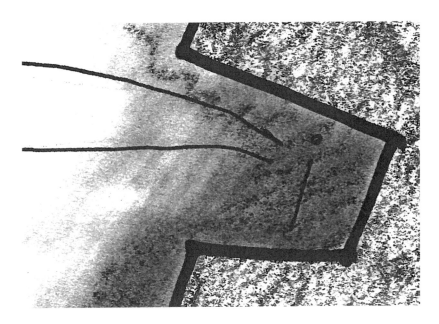

4

Places to Practice Designed Leadership

"A place belongs forever to whoever claims it hardest, remembers it most obsessively, wrenches it from itself, shapes it, renders it, loves it so radically that he remakes it in his own image."

—JOAN DIDION, *THE WHITE ALBUM*, 1979

"Consciously or not, we feel and internalize what the space tells us about how to work. When you walk into most offices, the space tells you that it's meant for a group of people to work alone. Closed-off desks sprout off of lonely hallways, and in a few obligatory conference rooms a huge table ensures that people are safely separated from one another."

—DAVID KELLEY, FOREWORD IN *MAKE SPACE: HOW TO SET THE STAGE FOR CREATIVE COLLABORATION*, 2011

HOW MUCH DOES PHYSICAL environment matter for learning, innovation, and leadership? Awareness of environment is often caught up in the nature-nurture debate. Why is it that some people, when led to a restaurant table in direct view of restrooms, almost on top of the serving station, and with their backs to a constantly opening and closing door, just stay put? They don't notice, don't care or, perhaps, don't want to kick up a fuss. Others of us are in the habit of seeking out the best possible space for our comfort and enjoyment, much to the chagrin of the maître d' who would prefer not to give us that perfect table.

Space and place matter for learning. They matter for business and policy innovation. And they certainly matter for designed leadership. In this chapter I focus on several aspects of a designed leadership environment—the studio, the lab, and the field—with their associated cultures of learning and experimentation.

Designated places, like studios or really any kind of differentiated spaces, are valuable for providing a focus for our mindset and for the activity intended. Sometimes, how we behave in various rooms in our houses or apartments are learned, sometimes it comes from a "design hint" (we behave in a certain way because of where the windows are, and also because certain aspects of our behavior are cultural). In some cultures, room use overlaps (sleeping, food preparation, eating); in other cultures we tend to separate activities.

In the case of differentiating thinking spaces, the key is to provide options. Ideally, there are spaces for solo thinking that are different from spaces designed for teamwork. This differentiation is important for designed leadership because we want to encourage certain types of behavior at certain times. For example, a room with no possibility for visual expression invites largely verbal behavior. A room lined with whiteboards or with lots of surfaces for writing and drawing invites visual expression. Designed leadership is about creating the best possible context to meet the needs of the moment. Space and comfort in that space is a critical component, often missed in our general consideration of leadership.

I grew up with a sort of studio in our house. It was my father's space, where he wrote, thought, invented, and read. He made his own desk out of knotty pine drawers on which he placed a varnished plywood top, maybe only one inch thick but with a nice edge to it. He set it up to look out at a foreground of garden, a middle ground of overgrown Vancouver Island blackberries and young maples, and a background of ocean, with the occasional ferry or fishing boat in view.

Interestingly enough, he also had a lab, of sorts, because he was a marine biologist—a clam and oyster guy who undertook both basic and applied research. Much of his work occurred in the field, generally in the intertidal zone where all of his favorite animals find their homes. But his lab was the place of controlled experiments, filled with equipment (mainly microscopes), lab benches, and specimens—sometimes live and sometimes in very smelly formaldehyde. I wish he were here so I could ask in which space he was the most creative. He might have said the field—where he undertook his most interesting and useful work, sitting on a raft, complete with a desk and microscope. It was here that he gave the signal that the time was right for the oyster industry to immerse their shell strings in the ocean because the oysters were about to spawn. The shells attracted the "spat" that grew into oysters. My father called it "mari-culture."

While I think he would have agreed with me about the creative influence of fieldwork, I doubt he would have called the space in our house his "studio," but it always had that feeling to me—so much so that when I had the chance to design my own studio for the first time,

I used my father's as precedent. Like his, mine faced the ocean—the Strait of Georgia between mainland British Columbia and Vancouver Island. I, too, used plywood to create a place to hide computers and printers, and a surface that gave me lots of layout space. The main difference was that my plywood was stained a purply pink color.

My first studio had a skylight, a skinny door to the deer-proof garden, and walls that I wrote on. I stuck pins into them all the time and I liked that none of this was precious. The studio just seemed to set the scene for openness and generosity. It was not a rigid place. It was what I needed it to be.

It also provided me with a particular context, a perspective from which I explored and appraised professional studios, labs, and field locations—thinking about their differences and similarities, and about how we can use them effectively in designed leadership.

Studios, Labs, and the Field

Studios and labs are proliferating as places of innovation, experimentation, and collaboration. In the teaching context, the Eberly

Center for Teaching Excellence and Educational Innovation at Carnegie Mellon University offers this definition: "Labs and studios provide opportunities for students to learn procedural skills in a setting where they can observe, practice, explore, solve problems (whether scientific or artistic), and gain mastery through hands-on use of disciplinary tools and techniques."[1] Similarly, labs and studios in business or government are often places of problem solving and practice.

Some might argue that labs and studios are the same thing, but I think they are different in both intent and usage. In general, the term "lab" signifies the scientific method—a more controlled, deductivist or top-down logical, hypothesis-testing approach to problem solving. Labs are places where you can conduct and control experiments that can be replicated and therefore promise results that will be accepted as "proven." The term "studio" tends to signify a more abductive approach where the emphasis is on open inquiry, asking plenty of questions, generating lots of possible solutions, trying them out and testing through prototyping. The studio approach generally begins with observation and then infers a theory or solution. Daved Barry and Stefan Meisiek, founders of Studio@CBS (the Copenhagen Business School) write in their paper, "Exploring the Business Studio," that, "[t]he term 'studio' derives from the Latin 'studium' (study, n), which early on evolved to mean a room for study (in Italian), and eventually, a place where learning happens through making."[2]

However, studios are just spaces until people make them places.

Most studios today are places of inquiry that emphasize craft, artistry, design, or some combination of these. "Studio" can describe both a place and a pedagogy.

While labs connote a more scientific tradition, studios come from the design and arts background. Barry and Meisiek go on to say: "To appreciate the difference between laboratory and studio, we need to accept that art making, designing, and crafting imply inquiry processes that have fundamentally different principles of operation than scientific inquiry, but that are nevertheless nonarbitrary, rigorous, and can be taught."[3]

Design thinking, strategic design, and new forms of problem solving have found their homes in labs and studios at universities and in business: MIT Media Lab in Boston, the former Helsinki Design Lab in Finland, Strategic Innovation Lab at OCAD University in Toronto, Institute Without Boundaries at School of Design, George Brown College, Social Innovation Lab at the Waterloo Institute for Social Innovation and Resilience, Weatherhead School of Management, Case Western Reserve University, D.School at Stanford, D.School in Potsdam, and a variety of business lab spaces in Procter & Gamble, SAP, and LEGO.[4] Governments are active, as well, starting with Denmark's MindLab, and now including the Policy Lab in the UK Cabinet Office, an Innovation Hub in the government of Canada's Privy Council Office, and numerous "intrapreneurship initiatives" in the offices of the provincial government of British Columbia.[5]

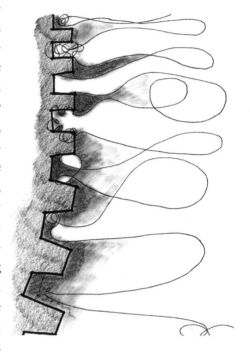

So studios have arrived as places for invention and reinvention, whether they are physical or virtual, and almost regardless of the medium or subject matter at hand.

I first arrived in a studio as a student of landscape architecture and design, an interdisciplinary profession that assesses performance based on a "crit," or critical review. The studio was a place where you worked, sometimes alone and for long hours. But it was also a place where your ideas were tested—perhaps moderated or improved by your colleagues or teachers.

Studio experiences are about enhancing our balance of critical and creative thinking and providing experiential learning. They are a place to practice our thinking and to think about our practices—a place of strategic design. A place to work on designed leadership.

Think, for example, about Apple and Steve Jobs or Jony Ive (the Apple designer). They both did their best to turn the Apple workplace into a studio, a place where ideas bounced off the walls. And eventually decisions and money were made.

Studios are ideal problem-solving places, where people from all sectors come together to solve social problems or resolve business challenges, from product and service development to market delivery and policy innovation. The studio environment implies a familiarity with design processes and integrated outcomes. It's where real-world problems are redefined, reframed, and reconstructed, within a predetermined time frame and budget. Sometimes this is the Skunk Works project, or a place of intense, focused innovation, where the experiences of the multisectoral studio are applied to imaginative systemic change, to redefine commerce in terms of expectations for the future—and outcomes that will change the world.

The Field

Getting out of the studio is often as important as the studio itself. The emphasis on observation and learning through presence cannot be overstated. The field can also be an extension of the studio; it might be any place where you can discover and explore your problem or challenge—and perhaps try out your solutions. Sometimes the place to practice designed leadership is in the lunchroom, or in a colleague's office.

Business Studios

Studios at business schools generally offer students, faculty, and staff a physical and virtual collaborative space for applying design strategies to develop and prototype tools, processes, and activities. Studios in design schools differ, in that they are more often places where students settle in and make a nest.

The original d.studio[6] at the UBC Sauder School of Business was a space and program where the interaction between design strategies and business content occurred.

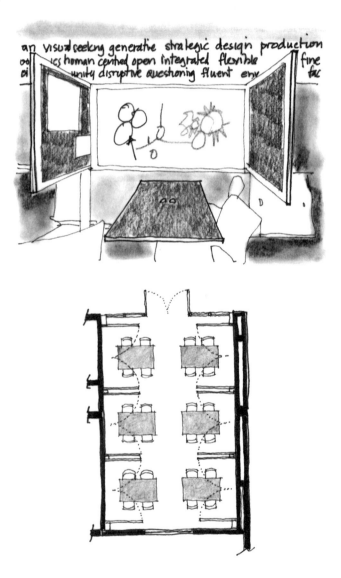

Sauder built the space in 2011, with a capacity of twenty students. It functioned as an action research studio to advance the practice of strategic design, as well as a teaching studio for undergraduate and MBA students.[7] But it immediately became popular for a variety of staff and faculty workshops. An increase in student numbers has necessitated moving the class to a larger studio with a different ambiance—as part of new Learning Labs at the Sauder Business School.

A design approach is being gradually introduced into the business school environment globally. There is a growing community of designers trying to understand how we can transform the business school experience using the concept of studio teaching to create a motivational and effective environment for learning business in all its complexities and rigor.[8]

Studios as Places

As places, studios generally share the following physical characteristics:

- lots of whiteboard space—either mobile or on the wall for drawing, erasing, and drawing again;
- lots of mobile furniture—ideally tables and chairs that move easily and can be instantly reconfigured depending on need;
- lots of light—ideally natural light—but often studio spaces, by economic necessity, are in low light spaces so good lighting is needed; and
- lots of storage space for "stuff"—prototyping materials, Post-its, pens, and so on.

Having visited and analyzed both, Barry and Meisiek compare the Sauder d.studio with Procter & Gamble's Clay Street Studio in Cincinnati. Clay Street is housed in an abandoned brewery, apart from corporate headquarters—its "rough-yet-finished" surroundings exhibit the "calculated uncut roughness" that characterizes many studios.[9]

> To use Clay Street, would-be P&G participants have to pass rather stringent requirements—they must present a problem that has proven unsolvable by other means and sequester themselves for up to 12 weeks, leaving their emails, cell phones, and personal/social lives behind. The dedicated Clay Street staff work with the problem and participants as well, pulling together creative materials and exercises that they think might inform and reframe the problem. Like a theater stage, the Clay Street space is converted into a particular place for a particular time, one that facilitates out-of-the-box inquiry in bespoke ways. Clay Street appears to work well.[10]

Barry and Meisiek don't commit as to whether the success of Clay Street is its environment or its methods. Place and process interact—and then you have to add people, both facilitators and participants. They are all important factors.

Barry and Meisiek then talk about our d.studio at the UBC Sauder Business School, including the effect of a stark difference in budget.

> She [Moura] and her staff managed to equip it with floor-to-ceiling whiteboards that, when opened, double as storage lockers; movable tables and chairs round out the space. Despite these modest surroundings, the d.studio seems to work at least as well as Clay Street; numerous courses, executive workshops, and events have been staged there and participants regularly praise their experiences and achieve notable outcomes. Would the d.studio work better if it were housed in Clay Street-like facilities? Maybe, but maybe not. While the d.studio could not be more physically different than Clay Street, it nevertheless stands out as an example of successful

bricolage and effectuation[11], where significant somethings are regularly made out of practically nothing.[12]

Studio as Pedagogy and Process

If the place is important, so is the process. Barry and Meisiek point out that the right studio processes need to be in place for good inquiry and results. Whether a studio in a business or a "business" studio, as a type of pedagogy, studios share the following aspects:

- opportunities to practice "speaking visually," encouragement to draw ideas and to use drawings as part of discussion;
- active learning, where there is a balance of "theory moments" (short) and "practice follow-ups" (long)—studio pedagogy is about bridging theory and practice;
- a focus on balancing individual and team activities—acknowledgment that both are needed;
- building a studio culture—where critique and the sharing of ideas is part of the process and way of thinking; and
- exploring ways of thinking and communicating.

I mention studio culture and its importance, but note that culture gets reinvented with each group that inhabits a studio. They make it their own in many different ways.

Building on the conclusions that Barry and Meisiek have drawn from their work on "business studios," here are my thoughts around how to legitimize the studio—in a business, government, or education setting.

- *Ensure alignment with the business strategy through smart institutional positioning.* If the studio can be positioned to align with or, even better, support a business strategy, its value can be emphasized and leveraged. Trying to do something "outside the norm" to be "innovative" may not be perceived as good or successful positioning. This holds whether we are talking about a business school or a Fortune 500 business.

- *Find the right people to lead the studio.* Like many new-found (although old to some people) approaches, there is a tendency for people to jump on the bandwagon and assume they have the skills to deliver. With studio learning, it is ideal to have a design background, or at least to apprentice with someone who does.

- *Seek support from the top and the bottom.* In the case of the Sauder d.studio, I was fortunate to have the support and energy of Dean Dan Muzyka—and I ended up with a lot of support from the business students who saw the value of the d.studio. Without a champion, it is tough to make headway.

- *Develop a studio-based research agenda (in the educational setting).* I received good advice from author Roberto Verganti when I was starting the Sauder d.studio.[13] He said that until we established a research agenda for design in business schools, we wouldn't be credible. With several PhD students now doing research on strategic design and innovation, I can see the value of this advice.

- *Engage interdisciplinary players for richer solutions and rewards.* When we started the d.studio class it was only open to third- and fourth-year Commerce students. While you might consider the mix of accounting majors and organizational behavior majors as a diverse group, they are still all business students. Today, we have a much more interdisciplinary class, where the ratio is twenty-four business students and twelve students from across the rest of campus—engineers, sociologists, and environmental designers. Perhaps predictably, I seek to instill in my business students the understanding that when they graduate into the workplace, they don't just work with business students.

There continue to be many questions. For example, how does studio culture support best practices in the future workplace of students?[14] What is the language used in studio conversations?[15] What are the various ways that design is represented in the studio, depending on geography, discipline, or media?[16] How can reflective practice be encouraged in studios through techniques that are instructor-centered, student-centered, interactive, or experiential?[17] How can we measure a studio's contribution to collaborative practice?[18]

My colleague Angèle Beausoleil has researched and reported on the power of the studio in a d.studio case study. She analyzed sixty-four student reflection blogs about their d.studio experiences. Angèle did an analysis that combines qualitative source data (descriptive text) with quantitative data (word occurrence and phrase structure) that highlights the d.studio experience using the top twenty-five most frequently used words extracted from sixty-four reflection blogs ranked from highest to lowest occurrence.[19]

Angèle's work reveals both the frustrations of the studio participants (ambiguity, confusing process, and team conflicts) as well as the positive outcomes (place-based learning, peer-based learning, fresh and engaging learning experience). Angèle concludes:

Overwhelmingly, all students described their experience as learning about the principles of teamwork, design thinking and quality solutions. Many reflected that learning by doing leads to a new awareness that creativity can be learned and that conflict can lead to better solutions. The studio environment helped students debate, critique, and identify real-world problems. The one-room open space with movable tables and chairs facilitated the practice of techniques and tools resulting in transformed thinking styles associated with creative problem-solving. One student reflected, *"I learned that while design thinking is exactly what business needs, it is also exactly what business does not have time for."*[20]

Many studio education experiments continue with virtual design studios,[21] course conversions from lecture-based to studio-based in computer sciences at Monash University,[22] and the Columbia Design Challenge: Confronting the Ebola Crisis.[23] Inspired by Columbia, UBC launched a design challenge in fall 2015 where interdisciplinary undergraduate and graduate students worked together on a three-day project focused on finding solutions to water-management problems in global urban areas. They were introduced to the strategic design method and began practicing it during the challenge.[24]

Building on the experience of this challenge and the launch of our Masters of Public Policy and Global Affairs program, we are now shaping and experimenting with a Policy Studio in the Liu Institute for Global Issues.

As change becomes more unpredictable and rapid, we need to update our ways of developing and implementing policy. It is not enough to engage multidisciplinary "experts" in trying to address challenging problems; we need the energy, creativity, and insight of everyone who has a stake in an issue. And when we bring multisectoral actors together, a clear process framework is essential so there are results, not just more talk. The Policy Studio at the Liu Institute is built on the strategic design method where multidisciplinary teams blend creative and critical thinking techniques to cocreate, test, and launch resilient solutions. And, in this context, practice designed leadership.

Using our experience with using strategic design in studio environments to work on business problems, it has motivated us to create the Policy Studio at the Liu, which is in start-up mode to tackle policy innovation. A Policy Studio:

- focuses on complex and wicked systemic problems;
- has a global/international orientation;
- is oriented around the public good;
- is solution-oriented—emphasizing policy design, development and, most important, implementation; and
- has a strategic focus on academic research, including policy design research, policy learning research, civic participation research, and development of alternative methods of academic inquiry.

At this point, I need to admit to an additional bias. To me, studios are magical spaces. I grew up, that is, matured, and spent formative years in the landscape architecture studios at the University of Guelph and, subsequently, at the University of California, Berkeley. This is where I learned both discipline and freedom. This is where I watched my peers change and grow. And I watched it all inside the studio.

And now, in the studios I inhabit with students from all across campus, I see the same kind of magic.

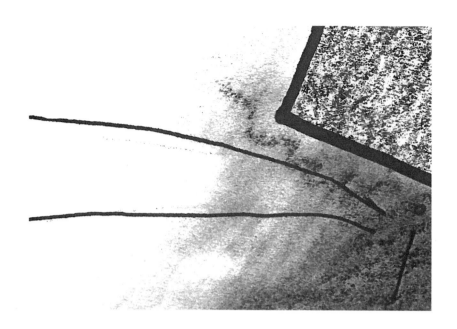

5

Learning and Education for
Designed Leadership

"Leadership and learning are indispensable to each other."

—JOHN F. KENNEDY, REMARKS PREPARED FOR DELIVERY AT THE TRADE MART IN
DALLAS, NOVEMBER 22, 1963 (UNDELIVERED)

"The illiterate of the 21st century will not be those who cannot read
and write, but those who cannot learn, unlearn, and relearn."

—ALVIN TOFFLER, *FUTURE SHOCK*, 1970

"I'm a better leader after I teach."

—ED BETOF, IN *TRAINING MAGAZINE*, JULY 2004

IN THIS CHAPTER I EMPHASIZE the importance of continual learning and education for leadership and explore the value that designed leadership brings to the leader as learner, mentor, and teacher. Leaders should act and simultaneously learn about others and about themselves. This learning can happen in many situations—in the workplace itself and also in b.schools (business), d.schools (design), and c.schools (creative leadership).

Being a student or learner at any time in our lives reminds us what it is like to learn how to do something new. Vulnerability and risk prevail when we step into something novel or outside of previous experience. Being a learner helps us to reflect on our learning processes and allows us to be more empathetic to others, who may also be in a learning process—either formal or informal.

Learning humbles us. The combination of psychological stresses and physical learning increases the challenge. For example, I learned to ride a motorcycle at age fifty and was constantly overintellectualizing the simple task of keeping the motorcycle upright. I had, perhaps, forgotten earlier experiences about simply doing. Psychological stress (*Will I drop the bike? Will I fall? Will I fail this simple task?*) and physical learning combined, and I overcame the challenge. As Aristotle wrote: "For the things we have to learn before we can do them, we learn by doing them."[1]

The Advanced Management Program at INSEAD challenged me to be a learner for a whole month, in a setting with seventy-nine other senior executives from around the globe. Peer learning may be one of the most powerful learning experiences. I remember a fellow INSEAD student with accounting expertise sitting me down and saying that we would not be leaving until I understood and could use the concept of *net present value*.[2] Openness to all types of learning and a willingness to be vulnerable is an important characteristic of designed leadership.

Reflection and Learning

There are many questions at the heart of this idea that leaders are learners, and learners are leaders. How does a leader act and simultaneously learn? This speaks to the importance of reflection and is backed up by the work of Donald Schön in *The Reflective Practitioner: How Professionals Think in Action*.[3] Schön's work focused on the architecture, psychotherapy, city planning, and science-based professions—exploring the role of reflection in what professionals do. In studying leaders as reflective practitioners, Schön talks about reflection in action and reflection on action.

The former is sometimes described as "thinking on our feet." It involves looking to our experiences, connecting with our feelings, and attending to our theories in use. It entails building new understandings to inform our actions in the situation that is unfolding. Practitioners allow themselves to experience surprise, puzzlement, or confusion in a situation that is uncertain or unique. They reflect on the phenomenon before them and on the prior understandings that has been implicit in their behavior.[4]

Reflection on action is something that practitioners engage in after a particular event or encounter. The act of reflecting on action enables us to spend time exploring why we acted as we did, what was happening in a group, and so on. In so doing we develop sets of questions and ideas about our activities and practice.[5]

When leaders combine reflection in and on action, they are in an active learning mode, which then informs and supports various roles: as continual learners, as engaged teachers, and as inspirational mentors. All of these roles utilize, at one time or another, the act of informed reflection—a key characteristic of designed leadership.

Informed Reflection

Talula Cartwright from the Centre for Creative Leadership writes: "Reflection may not seem like the right approach for leaders who are accustomed to taking action, but it is. It's a useful—even an essential—tool for those who want to be well-rounded, creative leaders."[6]

Rome's first emperor, Augustus, famously said *festina lente*: "hasten slowly." This means take action, but always in a prepared way, never rashly.[7]

The lesson here is: not so fast. Change and transformation are not amateur sports; you need to make time for the reflection required for designed leadership—leadership that makes a difference. It takes time to think, reflect, and then do.

It is difficult to find enough time in your day to integrate the critical, analytical thinking and the creative thinking that can give you energy and perspective. Sometimes reflecting alone is best, while other situations call for a sounding board of one or more colleagues.

My car conversations with Barry McBride is an example of one way to fit informed reflection into the day by reallocating

When I was involved in the evolution of a new campus for the University of British Columbia, the speed and intensity of the change process left too little time for reflection.

It was an unusual situation, because the team was living in the same hotel during key parts of the early process. Breakfast and dinner became times for integration and reflection. At dinner people would muse on the issues of the day. These would be discussed and reflected upon and then re-engaged again at breakfast or in the car on the way to the university campus.

Time in the car was also how Barry McBride and I managed our critical and creative discussions. Barry—the first deputy vice chancellor of UBC Okanagan—was a busy guy. He was the front man for the university in both the external community and within the growing academic community that we were evolving into UBC Okanagan.

The challenge for me was finding time with Barry to talk strategy. It turned out that the best time for creative, strategic thinking was in the car. It so happened that we were fairly frequently on the road up and down the Okanagan Valley, holding town hall meetings and other engagements with the community. This provided opportunities for miles of thinking.

Barry liked to drive, so he was relaxed and in an open and generative mood. I hate driving, but I can be a good passenger. I would have my list of topics, and we would use this time to productively strategize next steps, and to tackle some of the incredibly wicked problems that faced us daily during the transition process.

time that may otherwise be spent on chitchat. I think this particular approach works because the movement of the car and its privacy make the environment a focused one. There is something freeing about moving through the landscape that allows you both to dream big and imagine the impossible one minute and come down to earth and critique your ideas the next.

It is also a welcome time for learning and sharing—discussing what it means to lead a group of colleagues into the unknown. Such an opportunity is just one example of purposeful reflection with an objective in mind. The practice of informed reflection encourages post-project learning that involves taking the most from your experience and actively reflecting either individually or in a team about what you learned. My colleague Doug Paterson and I wrote about the importance of reflection in the design process and in design learning: "Reflection is the reconsideration of an idea or experience. Consciousness, retrospection, introspection, and self-knowledge are facets of the reflective act."[8]

Reflection can sometimes be helped by changing our mindsets—moving back and forth between critical and creative frames. In *Mindset: The New Psychology of Success*, Carol Dweck writes: "Mindsets frame the running account that's taking place in people's heads. They guide the whole interpretation process."[9] Dweck cites two types of mindsets: fixed and growth. Fixed mindset is focused on judging, while growth mindset is more focused on the implications for learning and improvement. The growth mindset is a better one for designed leadership.

Asking questions of oneself and others creates a more interactive reflective process. Role-playing, gaming, and changing one's context are also very valuable as a set of techniques for informed reflection. Yet another perspective is the outsight principle, from Herminia Ibarra in her recent book *Act Like a Leader, Think Like a Leader*. The outsight principle holds that:

> the only way to think like a leader is to first act: to plunge yourself into new projects and activities, interact with very different kinds of people, and experiment with unfamiliar ways of getting things done. Outsight, much more than reflection, lets you reshape your image of what you can do and what is worth doing.[10]

The outsight principle is another way of expressing informed reflection: it is purposeful, intentional, and future-oriented.

Reflection turns experience into learning.[11] In David Walker's chapter on "Writing and Reflection" in *Reflection: Turning Experience into Learning*, I was interested to discover research on the role of writing in learning. In a writing process course I took at the beginning of my academic career, I learned that during a writing project, you should spend about 30 percent of the time on "invention" (when freewriting comes in handy), about 20 percent on drafting, and a full 50 percent of your time on revision.[12]

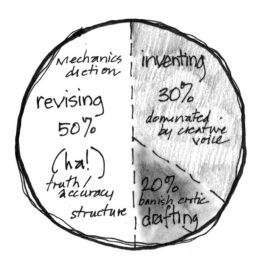

I have used that framework as a way of helping students learn about the design process through their writing process. After all, everyone *has* a writing process—or at least is able to identify one when asked—however chaotic it might be. I reported on this writing process-design process experience in "Using Writing Techniques in the Design Studio."[13] Five techniques stand out as useful for application around learning designed leadership: free-writing/free-drawing, dear critic, heuristics, clustering and branching, and word games.

Walker emphasizes the notion of writing as a tool for learning and reflection as he talks about keeping a portfolio to record learning experiences and to foster reflection. We now talk about e-portfolios as a way for students to build their repertoire of learning, some of which is in informal or unusual settings. Walker writes, "the word portfolio means a workbook, a forum within which one works seriously with the experiences of learning or life. It fosters that important and essential counterpart of experience: reflection."[15] Informed reflection is a central activity for continual learning, and consequently for designed leadership.

Five Techniques for Learning Designed Leadership

Free-writing is a writing process in which you generate ideas and practice silencing your critical voice to let your creative voice speak. Write whatever comes to mind, whether it is on the subject or not. Keep writing for a minimum of ten minutes. You'll be surprised what you generate.

Free-drawing invites you to express things that you see or feel in a nonverbal language while also silencing your critical voice. Choose media that are appealing to you. Draw lines. Let your drawing implement move where it wants to go. Don't be literal. This is not about being an artist. This is about "exercising" an often little-used part of your brain.

Dear critic asks us to recognize our inner critic. Give him or her a name, and even write a letter politely (or not) asking your critic to be quiet. We all have both critical and creative voices. Our critical voices are usually the strongest. This idea comes from Klauser in a chapter on the "Caliban Critic."[14] For designed leadership, the silencing of the inner critic at pivotal moments is essential.

Invention heuristics are useful in all sorts of processes. They are "rules of thumb" that we can apply to make decisions of all sorts. There are many invention heuristics that are useful for designed leadership, for example, definition and comparison. We can invent a list of questions that we can use frequently to help us generate or evaluate ideas.

Clustering and Branching (aka Mind Mapping) is a useful technique for visually organizing ideas or information or for mapping your thinking process. The process allows you to make connections and add new ideas that show relationships and, subsequently, lead to new ideas.

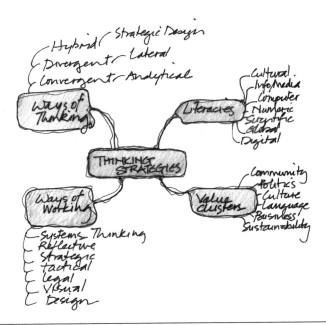

Continual Learning and Designed Leadership

In a learning organization, everyone is a leader in some way, and in their particular position in an organization. A 1994 conversation between Bruce Lloyd, a strategic-business professor at London South Bank University, and Fiona Bateson, then with Harbridge Consulting Group, explored the idea of "not one leader" as a way to host what they call transformational leadership.[16] "If the organization itself is well equipped to manage change," Lloyd says, "then not only is it being effectively managed but it is infused with an overall leadership culture which need not necessarily be identified with a leadership figurehead." Bateson adds, "One person might be the catalyst; they get the core of the idea but they need to manage the processes of testing it out within the organization, bouncing it around, involving many people in the process of honing both the idea itself, and the strategic process whereby it can be implemented." Bateson and Lloyd's ideas demonstrate the direct link to strategic design at the core of designed leadership.

Another vital question is, How do leaders (not just the C-suite) learn, especially as they are pivotal to creating learning organizations? To this, Bateson says,

> A lot of that has to do with the make-up of the particular individuals concerned at the moment, because we are not very successful at teaching leadership. We could be, but we are not. We are too dependent on people who, almost by chance, happen to be in the right place at the right time. If we are lucky, those involved have an open mind, are motivated by the right things, can cope with failure, and can live with responsibility in themselves and other people. Essentially leaders today need to understand themselves very well, before they are in a position to understand others.

The idea of designed leadership is that leaders have a tool kit that helps them be continual learners—both introspective and extrospective—with an open mind and generative ideas. Leaders with a design tool kit are always checking in on themselves and their teams, ideally using a personal or team strengths-weaknesses-opportunities-threats (SWOT) technique. This technique allows us to reflect on our strengths and weaknesses and on what is changing in terms of opportunities and threats. But continual learning can happen in many different ways, in varying relationships. One example is when the leader takes on the role of mentor or coach.

These are examples from the UBC Design Challenge—teams worked on personal and team SWOTs as part of warming up for the challenge.[17]

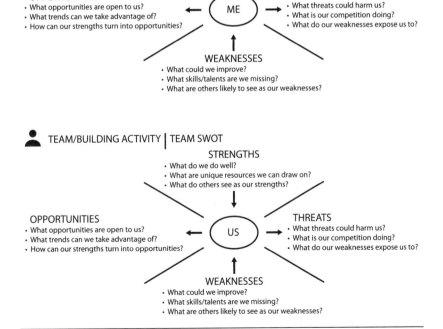

Inspirational Mentoring/Catalytic Coaching:
A Rich Learning Exchange

The designed leadership mindset is one that is open to coaching and being coached. There are few ways to better learn about oneself than to be a good listener for someone else.

Many leaders are mentors or coaches, while other leaders may teach, which has a more formal connotation than mentoring. Some leaders hold formal sessions where they are imparting information, but the most powerful learning for the mentee and the protégé is through an evolving mentoring process.

Mentoring and coaching are different. An organization called Management Mentors has identified twenty-five ways in which mentoring and coaching differ.[18] Coaching is more task-oriented and short-term, while mentoring is relationship-oriented and long term. No doubt, there are gray areas where coaching and mentoring characteristics overlap. What is more important is deciding when to consider a coaching system or a mentoring system in an organization. Coaching would certainly work when leaders need to acquire some new skills (like strategic design), and mentoring is useful when an organization is seeking to support or instill balance between professional and personal lives.

Mentoring allows people to learn while doing, which is a key characteristic of strategic design. Mentoring develops talent and creates the learning organization. Insala is a company that develops talent development software for employee development. They support mentoring and provide a rationale for leaders as mentors.[19]

> Leaders have a vision and the ability to get people around them to buy into the vision and achieve a result. The mentor functions like a leader by having the protégé believe and achieve the goals the mentor and protégé agree upon. The mentor's vision is seeing the protégé reach their potential and having the protégé believe in a plan to reach the goal. Leadership and mentoring go well together.[20]

Mentoring and coaching provide leaders with an opportunity for informed reflection, and can emphasize the process of learning leadership.

Where to Learn Leadership?

There is considerable debate about where leaders can best learn about leadership. *Monocle Magazine* publishes interviews with business leaders; they frequently ask whether leaders recommend an MBA program as a key prerequisite or whether business acumen best comes from experience. Sir Rod Eddington, former CEO of JP Morgan Australia responds, "On-the-job training really matters but whether you do an MBA or not it's important you get exposure to the most recent academic thinking."[21]

A Brief History of Business Education

Business education at the postsecondary level began as a practical degree, and was mainly viewed as a vocational or trade school discipline. By 1928, when the first PhD in business graduated from the University of Chicago, business began to be viewed as a legitimate subject of scholarship. By the 1940s, scholarship and scientific research were gaining acceptance as important professional activities for business school professors. However, the debate continues on whether or not management has the true characteristics of a profession.[22]

While business has established itself as an academic discipline, there are still some disagreements about the delivery of business education. Critics write that higher business education is in a "state of turmoil."[23] "Calls are being made for business schools to move away from the scientific model toward the professional or clinical model, much like medical schools."[24] Contrast that with a recent *The Wall Street Journal* article that explores the value of a liberal arts education, and the "need [for] flexible thinkers with innovative ideas and a broad knowledge base derived from exposure to multiple disciplines."[25] In *Rethinking Undergraduate Business Education*, Professor Anne Colby and colleagues also speak about the merit of a liberal arts education, as well as the importance of critical and creative thinking in a complex world

---

full of wicked business and societal problems.[26] More evidence is building around the importance of diverse thinking strategies in business referencing again the 2011 IBM study finding creativity to be the number one skill needed for CEOs.

About 60 percent of CEOs polled cited creativity as the most important leadership quality, compared with 52 percent for integrity and 35 percent for global thinking. Creative leaders are more prepared to break with the status quo of industry, enterprise, and revenue models, and they are 81 percent more likely to rate innovation as a "crucial capability."[27]

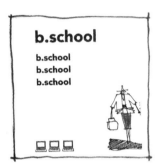

Given all the challenges facing business and society, more serious reflection and change is required in the halls of our business schools. Perhaps a greater integration of a design school model hybridized with the business school model could be a step in the right direction.

Most business schools market themselves as places to learn leadership. Harvard Business School invites students into "two years of leadership practice immersed in real-world challenges." [28] At Duke they say: "The world needs leaders of consequence."[29] Business schools started teaching leadership explicitly in the 1970s. In 1977, Professor Abraham Zaleznik published an intriguing paper titled "Managers and Leaders: Are They Different?" In 2004, Zaleznik's differentiation was succinctly summarized by an editor as:

The difference between managers and leaders, he wrote, lies in the conceptions they hold, deep in their psyches, of chaos and order. Managers embrace process, seek stability and control, and instinctively try to resolve problems quickly—sometimes before they fully understand a problem's significance. Leaders, in contrast, tolerate chaos and lack of structure and are willing to delay closure in order to understand the issues more fully. In this way, Zaleznik argued, business leaders have much more in common with artists, scientists, and other creative thinkers than they do with managers. Organizations need both managers and leaders to succeed, but developing both requires a reduced focus on logic and strategic exercises in favor of an environment where creativity and imagination are permitted to flourish.[30]

Designed leadership, or at least various facets of it, belongs in both the leadership and management camps. Managers also need to defer judgment and exercise their creative minds. This raises a question about what is taught in business schools and whether we need managers, leaders, or a hybrid skill set where everyone exhibits leadership qualities, even if their role may be defined as management. Opportunities to learn about managing and leading are expanding beyond the boundaries of business schools as more evidence mounts about the flexible, adaptable liberal arts graduates who are productively gracing global boardrooms. One of the reasons for this is the power of the edge and the boundary, where the overlap of disciplines and perspectives are the greatest.

Edge and boundary conditions in nature provide the richest and most diverse ecological habitats for plant and animal species (Principle 4). Designers, in business schools or anywhere outside of their natural habitat, live on the edge of their disciplines. Their interest is in the overlapping edges between business and design. A growing number of studios now exist in business schools, providing students and professors alike with places to explore the edges. Similarly, we are noticing the growth of studio environments in workplaces—making it even more important for students to be ready to engage and be productive in a new work environment.

Contrasted with the institutional history of business schools, the education of designers has historically been practice-based. Whether through apprenticeship or studio models, the learning is student-centered and focused on practicing the skills needed to become a professional.

Here is a list of postsecondary business studios that I am aware of:

- Business and Design Lab, Gothenburg University, Sweden
- Design Zone 125, F.W. Olin Graduate School of Business, Babson College, United States
- D.School, Stanford University, United States
- Stanley Wang D.School at National Taiwan University, Taipei, Taiwan
- Design Works, Rotman School of Management, University of Toronto, Canada
- Digital Business Studio at Jönköping University, Sweden
- K-Lab, ESSEC Business School, France
- HPI School of Design Thinking, University of Potsdam, Germany
- Manage by Designing, Weatherhead School of Management at Case Western Reserve University, United States
- Sauder d.studio, Sauder School of Business at the University of British Columbia, Canada
- Studio@CBS, Copenhagen Business School, Denmark
- Studio at C. B. D., University of Sydney Business School, Australia
- The Design Factory, Aalto University, Finland

A Brief History of Design Education

Design education traces its roots to the medieval guild, where artists studied under masters to learn a trade. In the 1900s, during the Paris Beaux Arts movement, design students worked under the guidance of a teacher or mentor on a design problem by "doing" the work of a professional.[31] Later influences on studio education came from the German Bauhaus movement, when instruction took a turn toward the practical for more technical aspects of design. New teaching models are still being developed, but the project-based system seems to sustain its power as a foundation for the traditional design disciplines.[32] The physical space of a studio provides a dedicated, collaborative workspace where students learn from each other as well as from expert advisors.[33]

As a designer in a business school, I am interested in transforming the concept of studio teaching into an effective motivational environment for learning business in all of its complexities and rigor.

During the typical education in most design disciplines (with the possible exception of industrial design), there is not much thought given to providing a specific business skill set. Courses in professional practice

litter the landscape, but do not profoundly influence budding designers, despite the practical and professional importance of the content. Studios are the places where passion for design, in whatever form, plays out. The challenge is for design schools to think about new ways to integrate business knowledge into their students' learning outcomes.

Both design and business school learning environments and student experiences vary dramatically with instructor, student, and circumstance. While there are many examples of effective teaching and learning, the business school teaching culture often remains focused primarily on the professor. And very often students prefer this model because it is less work for them. Enter the concept of business education through a design lens. Studios are places of praxis and innovation; the business studio opens opportunities for a different business learning style, in the classroom and in the workplace.

As the business environment becomes more unpredictable, organizations demand leaders who are capable of making the most of opportunities. Diverse interests, duties, and opportunities in today's markets mean that "better" is an increasingly complex concept. Providing students with a tool kit of diverse thinking strategies—including design—will create a greater capacity for innovation in the workplace. Sustained success is likely to occur within organizational cultures that value research, design literacy, design strategy, skills training, values-based evaluation, reinvention, and renewal. Leadership increasingly means being comfortable managing and motivating diverse teams of creative people. Truly innovative disruptive technologies and processes are needed to address the world's problems. One of the key attributes of designed leadership education—at whatever level—is learning integration. The basic skills to be developed include research, sketching, prototyping, collaborating, storytelling, and empathizing with clients, users, customers, and citizens. Studio learning environments are particularly well positioned to provide the skills that students need in this unpredictable world. But the integration of studios in business schools and the number of students who can benefit from the experience is difficult to scale up. Enter the creative leadership school.

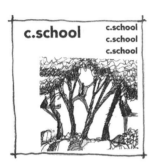

Business schools have their challenges and only the rare design school teaches leadership. Perhaps there is room for a hybrid model that promotes and nurtures designed leadership. As the traditional design and business school approach to leadership education continues to evolve, a new breed of schools is entering the marketplace. One example is THNK: School for Creative Leadership. THNK's mission is to "accelerate the development of creative leaders from across corporate, private, public, and social sectors and from all over the world. Together, we create innovative solutions to the world's most pressing and inspiring challenges."[34]

The school is based on the hybridization of business school and design school—promoting instead a "c-school" curriculum of innovation strategy, business-design thinking, leadership development, entrepreneurial mindset, and triple bottom line (recognizing not just financial, but also social and ecological evaluation). In 2014, the privately owned and funded THNK, based in Amsterdam, added schools in Vancouver, Canada and Lisbon, Portugal. The idea is to "catch" the next generation of creative leaders and challenge them with a part-time program that fits their lifestyles and gives them "real-life and inspiring topics of social relevance" to work on.

With the evolution of business thinking, as increasingly shaped by design, it is useful to investigate the design advantage: How does design interact with business and help its bottom line—ideally, its triple bottom line?

The Design Advantage for Business

 What is the advantage of using design and design strategies in business? The easiest argument focuses on return on investment (ROI). The UK Design Council has studied the value added by design, and in 2007, found that only 13 percent, or one in eight, companies actually measure their return on design investment.[35] However, those that do report a return of 15 percent. That said, it is difficult to determine what types of design investment are being measured: What is return? What is investment? Another study from Finland in 2011 and 2012, called the Design ROI Project, set out to develop a model and metrics to measure ROI in design. DROI-Measurable Design is a summary of the information gathered, the main finding, and the solutions developed.[36]

While ROI is important—and difficult to measure—there are other less-tangible parts of the design advantage. Design strategies help us blend the best of our creative and critical thinking skills. They provide techniques and thinking strategies to ask really good questions in the process of problem definition. Design welcomes ambiguity and provides the capacity for disruptive innovation while working within real-world constraints. Design disciplines challenge us to generate a multitude of solutions and then use good sifting, sorting, and sieving processes to get to the best one. Design produces tangible, tested outcomes—partly by encouraging experimentation and rapid prototyping. It focuses on humans, not organizations, through including users as codesigners. The process is generally team-based and fosters the collaboration of diverse disciplines and stakeholders. Design combines deep inquiry and agile decision-making, helps mitigate business risk, and is embedded in making good business decisions. Using design strategies in the competitive marketplace creates a business advantage.

Always a Learner

Designed leadership is based on the idea of continual learning. The strategic design process is all about asking questions, trying out ideas, and taking risks through the learning process. Having a strategic design mindset, being in ASK mode as much as possible, ensures openness to new ideas and different perspectives. Be open to learning every day, always a learner.

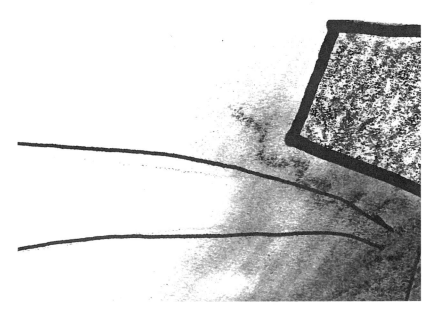

6

Designed Leadership Cases

"Collaboration begins with mutual understanding and respect."

—RON GARAN, *THE ORBITAL PERSPECTIVE: LESSONS IN SEEING THE BIG PICTURE FROM A JOURNEY OF 71 MILLION MILES*, 2015

RON GARAN IS JUST ONE of many people in the leadership research and practice community who argue that leadership is a group effort. Effective leadership arises more consistently from within teams when all members consider themselves leaders working together, rather than answering unquestioningly to a voice from the top.

David Pendleton, from the Said Business School at Oxford, writes:

> Complete leadership is more likely to come from several people acting together as a complementary team than from one individual acting alone. The best leaders are not well rounded—but the best teams are.[1]

Jean Woodall, from the Westminster Business School, writes:

There is still a tendency to see the leader as a heroic individual at the top of the organization. Action-centered leadership, situational leadership, transformational leadership, authentic leadership, and servant leadership—there is a long tradition of fads for how a leader should behave. All these different approaches to leadership are more about being rather than doing. Yet practicing managers are ill-advised to take their eye off doing. . . . So no more heroes, fads or formulae in leadership please.[2]

Miki Kashton, from *The New York Times*, writes:

When leaders commit to involving the whole group, organizations are transformed. Although collaboration—or "laboring together" (*collaborare* in Latin) isn't easy, it becomes easier the more we welcome difference and even conflict in service of a larger whole. The results are higher trust, increased productivity, and rich creativity.[3]

Designed leadership is about utilizing the diversity of thinking that surrounds us. It seems to lose all energy and effect when considered as a fad or formula, if only because these things tend to narrow and deny in the name of focus, rather than admit the myriad influences of which the leader may take advantage. We can utilize a diverse range of thinking strategies to approach any problem or opportunity. The challenge of knowledge integration across disciplines that we face in most situations is no different. There is potential to use design in its broadest terms to invent a collaborative and transformative opportunity that mobilizes knowledge by closing the gaps between producers and consumers. While this book is about designed leadership, I hope it will also encourage the use of the strategic design method in many realms of activity—especially as a learning process.

Three cases follow that illustrate the collaborative aspects of designed leadership: The Campus City Collaborative; Leading Cities; and the Pacific Coast Collaborative. These examples also embody varying degrees of success in integrating the concept of collaboration among academia, business, government, nonprofits, and civil society.

These collaborative cases refer less to when and how we are creative, and more to the importance of collaboration and the exchange of ideas, voices, and experience when solving wicked problems. It is about disciplines exchanging ideas and approaches as part of designed leadership.

The Campus City Collaborative

Early in 2009, the new mayor of Vancouver, Gregor Robertson, announced that he wanted his city to be the greenest in the world by 2020. Everyone from Robertson's staunchest local critics to former New York Mayor Bill de Blasio were watching the process. Robertson's first initiative was to launch the Greenest City Action Team (GCAT), for which he recruited fourteen people (including me) with experience in urban environment and economy; he challenged us to gather best practices and ideas and then to make recommendations to the city council.

In May 2009, the team sent its first report to the city council. It was called *Quick Start* (in name and process) and proposed forty-four actions within three policy areas: jobs and the economy, greener community infrastructure, and human health.[4] Work then continued on longer-term recommendations and targets. *Vancouver 2020: A Bright Green Future* was released in October 2009. It identifies ten long-term goals, supported by a set of measurable and attainable 2020 targets.[5]

Greenest City Goals

1 Green economy, green jobs

1. Gain international recognition as a mecca of green enterprises
2. Eliminate dependence on fossil fuels
3. Lead the world in green building design and construction

2 Greener communities

4. Make walking, cycling, and public transit preferred transportation options
5. Create zero waste
6. Provide incomparable access to green spaces, including the world's most spectacular urban forest
7. Achieve a one-planet ecological footprint

3 Human health

8. Enjoy the best drinking water of any major city in the world

9. Breathe the cleanest air of any major city in the world

10. Become a global leader in urban food system

Given these challenging goals and targets, implementation was critical. GCAT members were asked to find ways to continue their work with the city. The public servants became very engaged throughout the process, and many of them became champions for various initiatives. Two GCAT members, former Vancouver mayor and former British Columbia Premier Mike Harcourt and I, decided to take a proactive role in implementing one of our Bright Green ideas: building a collaboration between the city and the postsecondary sector.[6]

The Campus City Collaborative (C3) was born in late 2009. An informal group of academics from the city's six postsecondary institutions and key personnel from the City of Vancouver gathered to imagine ways to maximize synergy among ourselves and our organizations. Members included the City of Vancouver, the Vancouver Economic Commission, and Vancouver's six public postsecondary institutions.[7]

The initiative was designed to help the city tap into the burgeoning creativity and intelligence of its campuses to achieve its Greenest City Action Plan targets.

C3 presented an opportunity to demonstrate that, in Vancouver, things can be done differently. We can break down the disciplinary isolation in our institutions. We can collaborate more effectively while providing a real-world learning environment for students.

C3 was designed to create as many opportunities as possible for collaboration among postsecondary institutions and the city. In its first year, three catalyst projects were funded and launched: a Green Workforce Development Symposium, Carbon Talks, and CityStudio.

The Green Workforce Development Symposium was held to consider ways in which C3 institutions could meet the growing demand for education and training to equip workers for new types of green jobs. Carbon Talks, a program at Simon Fraser University, served as a platform to discuss, define, and manage the transition to a low-carbon economy.[8] Such an economy requires all sectors to collaborate and cocreate a city where talent is retained and green innovations are made. In 2012, Carbon Talks invited sixteen business leaders to discuss the opportunity to create a global urban sustainability center, thus drawing the business sector into a C3 process that had previously been confined to three partners: government, academia, and civil society.[9] At this gathering, we asked the question, What are the roles and needs of businesses in the development of Vancouver as a global center on urban sustainability? Conclusions from the Carbon Talks session included the need to rethink sustainability, including introducing some form of monitoring and reporting platform for businesses. We also identified the need for a revenue-generating business case for participation in an urban sustainability center; we were, and are, looking for concrete benefits for businesses.

While C3 and Carbon Talks were a good start on the business-connection front, we still lacked a project with legs. As is often the case, serendipity stepped up. The Greenest City program Talk Green to Us sponsored a mash-up, where projects were proposed and then voted upon by a social media audience. The most popular project was the concept of a studio in which undergraduate students would learn together while helping the Greenest City program demonstrate some of the greenest city goals. The program recognized the potential synergy this project would have with C3, and they launched CityStudio.

CityStudio . . . The City is the Classroom

CityStudio is an innovative program in which students and instructors from C3 institutions work together to address Vancouver-specific green goals.[10] Students enrolled in CityStudio (both a place and a conceptual, student-centered learning environment) receive credit at their host institutions. City staff and other experts provide background information to the program. Each postsecondary institution also develops specific partner courses that align with—and can be taught in conjunction with—the issue being addressed in CityStudio that term. These partnerships expanded student involvement from twenty students in the Core Studio to generally over three hundred students in partner courses in the postsecondary institutions.

- British Columbia Institute of Technology
- Emily Carr University of Art + Design
- Langara Community College
- City of Vancouver

- Vancouver Economic Commission
- University of British Columbia
- Vancouver Community College
- Simon Fraser University

CityStudio projects and course work emphasize sustainability leadership, social enterprise, education of change managers, and the development of green businesses. Early work focused on a single Vancouver neighborhood and on the implementation of demonstration projects involving access to nature, local food, and development of the green economy.

CITYSTUDIO

CityStudio has attracted multiyear funding, and continues to receive City of Vancouver support. The broad Campus City Collaborative (C3), on the other hand, was not sustained. The C3 concept was perhaps ahead of its time, in the sense that the sectors (academic-city-business) have a diverse set of cultures, timelines, and participants. While the concept of multisectoral collaboration is strongly endorsed everywhere, it is difficult to achieve. This said, C3 offers a host of lessons learned.

Collaborations involving local government, businesses, and academic institutions require certain conditions:

- Long-term Perspective: it takes time to achieve results.
- Student engagement: there is a difference between undergrad research (relatively easy to secure, but not as professional) and graduate research with professorial support (highly competent, but more difficult to secure).
- Relationships: the people involved can make it or break it.

The designed-leadership lens helped us focus on the importance of long-term thinking, the need for early engagement with multiple players, the importance of openness to different orientations and perspectives, and the need to work with people who have different mindsets, time frames, and agendas.

Despite the challenges, even modest, low-commitment engagement can be worthwhile in the sense that postsecondary institutions are eager for simple exchanges of information and regular relationship building. C3 revealed the need for a single point of contact. We needed reliable portals with a navigator who was also an accomplished networker. Networkers like to know what everyone is doing, to be able to quickly identify priorities, which can begin to be tackled through short-term research assignments. Cities that are interested in working with academic partners can also post information on subject areas where they are looking for research. Graduate students are always looking for research topics; if they see the need and the appetite (and a chance for some funding!), they are often in the perfect position to help develop simple protocols for city engagement of academics.

Given the lessons we learned from the Campus City Collaborative, I started looking for a way to continue its mandate in a more global environment. Leading Cities offers a unique opportunity to provide an international dimension.

Leading Cities

The World Class Cities Partnership was founded by members of the School of Public Policy and Urban Affairs at Northeastern University in Boston.[11] Recently, the name has been changed to Leading Cities. Leading Cities brings together cities and their universities to undertake urban policy research projects that draw on the experience of all member institutions.

LeadingCities

Global Impact on a Local Level

Leading Cities identifies and invites only one city per country to join, keeping the network small to allow development of strong research and practice relationships. Leading Cities is still in its infancy, doing new things in an exciting growth period. The program currently has the following founding members: Boston, Barcelona, Dublin, Hamburg, Lisbon, Lyon, Rio, Vancouver, and Zapopan/Guadalajara. Modest expansion into global south cities is anticipated in the next few years.

The Leading Cities program focuses on an annual joint research project, decided upon at an annual summit, guided by monthly conference calls, and finalized and prepared for publication at the following conference. Some member universities piloted connecting courses virtually in different cities to offer opportunities for students to interact. This also offered the opportunity to introduce potential research partnerships. Leading Cities has completed three research projects: *Talent Magnets: Cities and Universities Building the Workforce for a Knowledge Economy* (2012), *Exploring Co-Creation in Leading Cities* (2014), and *Co-Creation Connectivity: Addressing the Citizen Engagement Challenge* (2014).[12] The cities, though very different from each other,

have many similar issues and aspirations. European cities appear to have much to teach North American cities in areas such as advancing cultural industries, branding and promotion, digital strategies, and civic participation.

The 2012 research project on talent retention and attraction was lauded by American urban studies theorist Richard Florida in a tweet to his 150,000 followers.[13] Here is an excerpt from the executive summary that points to the need for leadership around city-university strategies:

> Despite the potential, no Leading City currently institutes a comprehensive collaboration strategy between universities and city government and other stakeholders. In fact, universities and cities often unintentionally work against talent retention. Many cities and universities lack strong student integration efforts prior to graduation. Student housing, for example, is often limited to the academic year, forcing students to leave the area during non-semester periods when they are most likely to build professional relationships through internships.[14]

The 2013–2014 topic of cocreation provided an opportunity for cities and their postsecondary institutions to share knowledge of experiments and case studies about citizen engagement and empowerment. The Vancouver offering was an experiment in cocreating a workable business model for electric vehicle charging. A group of MBA students worked with the City of Vancouver and a range of stakeholders to learn about challenges and

opportunities. The 2014–2015 follow-up project focused on cocreation connectivity and the challenge of citizen engagement.

Leading Cities is a good example of testing multisectoral leadership. While the focus in the beginning has necessarily been narrow—i.e., no business involvement—this is changing with a proposed governance model that will include local business advisory groups to the various Leading City chapters.

Of relevance to designed leadership is the learning that comes from engaging in codesign or cocreation. As leaders learn more, experiment, and practice, the value of engaging the multisectoral collaboration increases, as is evident in the case of the Pacific Coast Collaborative.

The Pacific Coast Collaborative

What do Arnold Schwarzenegger and Sarah Palin have in common? They were both governors when I became the BC commissioner of the Pacific Coast Collaborative.

The Pacific Coast Collaborative (PCC) is the creation of Gordon Campbell, premier of British Columbia from 2001 to 2011. Observing a distinct lack of collaboration among governments along the Pacific Coast, he used his persuasive powers to create a forum for cooperative action, leadership, and information sharing concerning issues affecting Pacific North America.

The objective was to help realize the aspirations of each Pacific Coast jurisdiction, especially when they required decisive action at the local, state, province, and national level to address issues like regional transportation, clean energy, sustainable economy, emergency management, research and innovation, and ocean health.

For the final year of my deputy minister appointment (2008–2009), I was asked to be the commissioner for a new initiative put forth by the premier of British Columbia and the governors of Alaska, Washington, Oregon, and California to position the region for the Pacific Century. The vision is to share leadership practices among government, businesses, and academia for cooperative action on five priorities affecting the Pacific coastal jurisdictions—home to 54 million people and a GDP of over $2.5 trillion.

The initial priorities were clean energy, regional transportation, sustainable regional economy, emergency management, and innovation, research, and development.

The BC Pacific Coast Collaborative Commission built the relationships and developed the agenda for the first meeting of the partners in February 2010. The commission's staff of five public servants worked toward this inaugural meeting. We visited each governor's office to develop a broad menu of ideas and actions that were of interest to the five partners. We used focus groups in each jurisdiction, bringing together thought leaders from business, academic, nonprofit, and governmental sectors.[15]

We analyzed the outcome and developed a short list that was then discussed with the partners via teleconference. Out of this process, we wrote *Vision 2030*, which aims to determine what our region could look like in 2030.

Vision 2030 is intended to serve as a living document for the Pacific Coast Collaborative,

Positioning Pacific North America
for Sustainable Prosperity

Released for comment and discussion by the Premier of British Columbia and the Governors of California, Oregon and Washington on the occasion of the first Leaders' Forum of the Pacific Coast Collaborative in Vancouver, B.C. on February 12, 2010.

providing a strategic vision for regional collaboration, to be refreshed and refined with new ideas and information in the coming years through engagement with our citizens. Out of the menu and vision process, we developed two action plans for the leaders to accept, which required getting buy-in from our public service partners. We worked to choose actions that were tangible and meaningful, not just rhetorical.

The four state governors and the BC premier, at their 2010 meeting, signed the 2030 vision statement, the *Action Plan on Ocean Conservation and Coastal Climate Change Adaptation* and the *Action Plan on Innovation, the Environment, and the Economy.* Subsequent to my involvement in the PCC, the partners have signed off on other work plans. More important, the staff in each of the governments continues to work collaboratively and build relationships on a number of key initiatives in areas important to the PCC.

The *West Coast Action Plan on Jobs* was signed by the PCC in 2012. Both politicians and public servants have been focused on implementing the 2012 action plan, including implementation of a West Coast Infrastructure Exchange (WCX).[16] California, Oregon, Washington, and British Columbia form the WCX, which was launched to "create and develop innovative new methods to finance and facilitate development of the infrastructure needed to improve the region's economic competitiveness, support jobs and families, and enhance our shared quality of life. It will rely on private sector expertise, stretch dollars further, and increase accountability." The Brookings Institution deemed the WCX a "2012 Governance Innovation to Watch."[17]

The governors and premier have met almost annually to approve and implement collaborative action plans. In October 2013, they announced the *Pacific Coast Action Plan on Climate and Energy*, with a set of shared goals for reducing carbon emissions and building a clean energy economy on the West Coast. Major goals include: (1) leading national and international policy on climate change; (2) transitioning the West Coast to clean modes of transportation and reducing the large share of greenhouse gas emissions from this sector; and (3) investing in clean energy and climate-resilient infrastructure. You can find more details in the PCC 2014 annual progress summary on the PCC webpage, including a list of commitments made.[18]

In May 2016, the West Coast governors and the BC premier made new commitments to advance subnational models for tackling climate change with an updated *Pacific Coast Action Plan on Climate and Energy* to match the bigger commitments to greenhouse gas reductions reflected in the Conference of the Parties (annual global climate conference) global climate change talks in Paris in December 2015. The action plan of 2016 has a stronger emphasis than in the past on issues including ocean acidification; the integration of clean energy into the power grid; support for efforts by the insurance industry and regulatory system to highlight the economic costs of climate change; and so-called super pollutants (also known as short-lived climate pollutants).[19]

It takes leadership at all levels to sustain something like the Pacific Coast Collaborative.[20]

While these types of government collaborations are not easy, the fact that the governments are working together is encouraging. This provides a hopeful example of resilience planning at the regional level.

Lessons Learned from the Collaborative Cases

There are many reasons why collaboration is challenging. Below are some suggestions from a report I wrote after the experience of chairing the City of Vancouver's Urban Landscape Task Force, titled *Greenways-Public Ways*.[21] I find the following lessons to be equally applicable to the three cases in this chapter.

We go fast to go slow. We are incredibly impatient. To collaborate at the scale of some of these examples involves negotiating numerous jurisdictions, policy mandates, political ambitions, and a ton of information that needs to be digested and synthesized. It takes time and careful strategic thought to advance collaboration, given the complexities we face and the time it takes to build working relationships.

We try to implement too many ideas at once. This was certainly the case with the Pacific Coast Collaborative. We had to be very strategic about which ideas might work in all jurisdictions. Focus was critical. The critical and creative lenses of designed leadership are constantly in play. On one hand, long-term thinking—generating a diverse range of options for the action plan that extended to 2030—was important; on the other hand, identifying constraints and targets that were aspirational but not crazy provided credibility to the plan.

We lack the ability to take risks. Any kind of multisectoral exploration is full of risks—personal, professional, and financial. However, the strategic design method, if implemented as part of designed leadership, helps to mitigate risks. The process of rapid prototyping and experimenting (fast and cheap) is one way to be able to learn about how risky an idea might be.

Turf wars and territoriality abound in any kind of collaborative project. People are protecting jobs they know, and they fear the unknown. Departmental or unit compartmentalization and lack of interdisciplinary thinking work against collaboration.

The general complexity of problems today challenges us. Look at this diagram of all the connections that we make to each other.

It takes time and energy, as well as confidence that the investment will be worthwhile, to connect to all these people and to sustain relationships.

Despite these challenges, finding creative solutions to mobilize knowledge is an important strategy. These cases continue to provide rich opportunities for transforming relationships and for helping to find ways of bridging knowledge mobilization gaps.

As with any good iterative design approach, we keep circling back to "What if?"

MQ Map.

UBC **Sander** School of Business

- Asia Pacific.
- UK / European Union
- City of Vancouver (Metro Vanc)
- Greenest City Action Team
- Ottawa - Federal etc Granting Councils
- Provincial Ministries MoE, EMPR, OGS, TRANS, TIDES
- VBoT
- BC Business Council
- Global Business Schools
- Global Design Schools
- Canada-Calif. Research Partnerships
- Pacific Coast Collaborative
- UC System / Cal State System
- NGOs - EcoTrust / Tides
- Philanthropic Org - Renewal

Faculties

U.B.C.
- Design Centre for Sustainability
- Geoff Atkins Sust. Leader (Pres Office)
- Centre for Clean Energy / HRC
- Charlene Easton Campus Sustain. Office
- Mike Harcourt in Continuing Studies

- Centre for Interactive Research on Sustainability
- BC Working Group on Sustainability Education

- SFU
- BC Post Secondary Institutions
- UVic
- BCIT

What if business is invited to pull up a chair to the Campus City Collaborative (C3) table? The C3 concept can be a success only if business becomes a key player with all the benefits.

What if the programmatic activities of C3 such as research symposia and green jobs conferences each became a dynamic vehicle for addressing the theory/practice gap, the communication and literacy gap, and the culture gap (see Principle 5)?

What if we create a new business model for C3 that reinvents the typical structure of a business start-up? What if the studio concept is adopted to better prepare students to be work ready? By engaging governments in innovative ways, postsecondary institutions can also develop new approaches to education and strengthen their offerings to researchers and students by giving them access to current urban challenges.[22]

Multisectoral approaches and the designed leadership frame create a working approach to tackle the varied challenges we face.

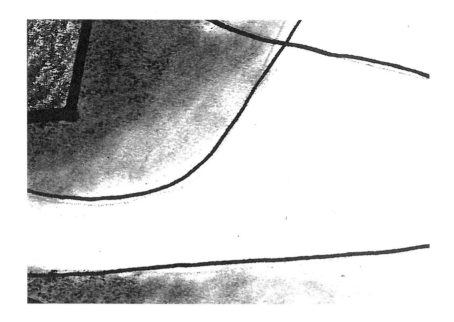

7

Take-Away

IT'S THE BOLD, perhaps overconfident writer who saves the best bits for last. At least, that's the advice I got from my writing mentor, Richard Littlemore. A newspaper veteran, Richard still believes that you should put the big news on the front page, lest your readers—short of time or attention—wander off before finding the good stuff.

But now that you're here (and whether you came page-by-page or in a leap), these are the points I hope you take away—the lessons I think are most important.

Take-Away 1: Strategic design and designed leadership are concepts to be used, hybridized, and played with. They are not silver bullets, nor are they simplistic recipes for great leadership or blustering formulas from the guaranteed-to-succeed, self-help book stacks. Strategic design (method and mindset) and designed leadership are ways of thinking that can open our minds to subtlety, as well as to revelation. They are invitations for you to value others' ideas and to be generous with your own. Designed leadership is about sharing and openness.

Take-Away 2: Experiment. Practice. Ask. Try. Do. After sampling this book you might occasionally wonder: Am I solving the right problem or asking the right question? Should I design a little experiment to test this idea? When you find yourself stuck or short of ideas, you might riffle through Ask, Try, Do, and see what happens.

Take-Away 3: Think visually. Any opportunity that comes along—practice your visual thinking skills. Trying to explain something? Draw it. Diagram it. Trying to think through a problem and opportunity? Reach for a pen or a crayon.

Take-Away 4: It takes time. Expect it. Organizational change is not for triflers or dilettantes—it is almost impossible to make change hastily or off the side of your desk. Change happens over time, often unnoticed and sometimes unwelcome. Good change generally requires a strategic nudge at the right moment—and a great font of patience and perseverance in the minutes, hours, days, months, seasons, and years that follow. If change is needed, don't wait—but don't rush.

Take-Away 5: It takes time. Honor it. People change over time, too. We mark time with lights (on and off); with urban barometers and time boards (clocks, market ticker tapes, Olympic countdowns); with autumn bonfires and summer fireworks; perhaps with swimming under the stars.[1] Yet marking time in leadership is often missed. There is good reason to pause and mark an occasion, and not just for big, public events, office moves, or seasonal parties. As a leader, you also need your own approach for regularly reflecting on your leadership. It might mean going for a walk each month or year at the same time in the same location. It could mean checking in with or engaging your team in a new way. It might mean changing your behavior. You need to take time to redesign the future. What has been working and why? What hasn't been working, and what can you do about it?

Take-Away 6: Clear, transparent, engaging, and well-communicated processes move us ahead. Change is most welcome—and ultimately most successful—when people can see it coming and recognize it for what it is. Successful processes also require a common language, one that people can use together in the unending quest for shared understanding. Designed leadership requires agile thinking, a focus on problem definition, and a willingness to question and to defer judgment. It also requires being comfortable with not having the right answer—which, again, demands clarity and transparency. Designed leadership practitioners have a vision and a contagious confidence—in part because they don't oversell.

Take-Away 7: Learning. What is it like to step into something completely unfamiliar? What is it like to take risks and be vulnerable? We know the answer: It's risky. It's frightening. And it's fabulous. It's where learning takes place—and it's where we need to be. Today's leaders need to be designing with twenty-first-century strategies. Old modes of thinking will produce the same old results. There's a new set of skills to be learned.

Appendix

The Evolution of Strategic Design in Business Thinking

"The history of commerce is the history of civilisation."

—HENRY DE BELTGENS GIBBINS, *THE HISTORY OF COMMERCE IN EUROPE*, 1891

FROM MY DAYS AS A LANDSCAPE architect and urban designer (in the eighties and nineties), then as an urban policy advisor, I brought a particular perspective to later leadership roles in helping to transform institutions and even sectors of advanced education, science, and technology. I realized that my strategic design approach was crafted to be accountable to a broad set of values.

In those days, business was often regarded as a relentless natural force of economic self-interest. Businesspeople and politicians were assumed to be well-informed and reasonable, and we thought we could rely confidently on the invisible hand of the markets to manage their complexity. Of course, that was too simplistic an approach, but the expectations of business decision making by regulators, the courts, and the media have added incrementally—and immeasurably—to the level of complexity since then. My experience and interest in leadership come directly from formative studies of design processes and decision making, supplemented by inquiring and creative minds in the business of business.

One such mind was Dr. Daniel Muzyka, then dean of the UBC Sauder School of Business. Dean Dan's international experience and entrepreneurial talents bridged both community and business practice.[1] I was at a point of transition, and we were chatting about my next career stage, when he said, "Wait a minute—you are a designer!" and then promptly invited me to join the Sauder School to introduce design into the business curriculum. A glass of wine later, I said yes.

A persistent lesson learned for me has to do with the common gaps I've recognized among government, business, and academia. In the strategic design method we often start with looking for a common language. As a deputy minister—the most senior public servant in the Canadian legislative system—I created an informal business advisory council for my work in the Ministry of Advanced Education. My experience with this group led me to realize how many great ideas are separated because we lack a common language and have vastly different vocations. The old separation of the business of business being money and the business of government being people were breaking down in a world where everything matters, from low carbon to high respect, from cost effectiveness to flash transactions. Perhaps the time had come to dust off a tool kit of thinking strategies and problem-solving processes, and enthusiasm to teach and learn complex decision making with future business leaders.

In my introduction, I suggested that we need to leap over three barriers—aimlessness, fear, and illiteracy—by learning to take direction, learning to take risks, and learning to get along. One of the ways of understanding the potential of the design-business connection is to delve into the history of business thinking and of how, recently, design has made its way into business itself, and specifically into thought on business leadership.

Pivot Points in Business Thinking
Through a Strategic Design Lens

Strategic design is concerned with maintaining movement and continual improvement toward a goal. In any change of direction or balance, it is a good idea to know what is behind you. The ideas of designed leadership and the strategic design method are based on the diverse thinking strategies that we need for success—whatever our objectives in life and work. I was excited to learn and work in systems of business, first as a small business owner and consultant and then, a generation later, in a leading business school. Yet increasingly I became aware of my own knowledge gaps and the need to develop reliable sources of ideas and trends. The history of business thinking is a good place to start. With the design lens, there is an opportunity to explore the evolution of business thinking and the influence of strategic design on business through the decades.

When did bookstores start featuring a business section? At Harvard, it was probably in 1927. Others would point to early books on business systems, such as Frederick Winslow Taylor's *The Principles of Scientific Management* (1911), or Henry Ford's writing (1922–1930) on production systems and observations on organizational behavior, or to Dale Carnegie's musings in 1936 on *How to Win Friends and Influence People*.[2] Taylor had been motivated after seeing the waste of natural resources and larger wastes of human effort through "blundering, ill-directed or inefficient" acts—what we now call "churn"—which created problems "less visible, less tangible and are but vaguely appreciated."[3]

One way to track the pivot points in the evolution of business thinking is to take a look at key business books through time, using a strategic design lens.

Game-Changing Business Books from the perspective of strategic design and designed leadership

Title	Author	Date
The Art of War	Sun Tzu	sixth century B.C.
The Prince	Machiavelli	1513
The Wealth of Nations	Adam Smith	1776
The Principles of Scientific Management	Frederick Winslow Taylor	1911
My Life and Work	Henry Ford	1922
How to Win Friends and Influence People	Dale Carnegie	1936
The Practice of Management	Peter F. Drucker	1954
Andrew Carnegie	Joseph Frazier Wall	1970
Manias, Panics, and Crashes: A History of Financial Crises	Charles P. Kindleberger	1978
Competitive Strategy: Techniques for Analyzing Industries and Competitors	Michael E. Porter	1980
The One-Minute Manager	Kenneth H. Blanchard and Spencer Johnson	1981
In Search of Excellence: Lessons from America's Best-Run Companies	Thomas J. Peters and Robert H. Waterman, Jr.	1982
The 7 Habits of Highly Effective People: Powerful Lessons in Personal Change	Stephen R. Covey	1989
The Fifth Discipline: The Art & Practice of the Learning Organization	Peter M. Senge	1990
Organizational Culture and Leadership	Edgar H. Schein	1992
Competing for the Future	Gary Hamel and C. K. Prahalad	1994
The Innovator's Dilemma: When New Technologies Cause Great Firms to Fail	Clayton M. Christensen	1997
The Tipping Point: How Little Things Can Make a Big Difference	Malcolm Gladwell	2000

Title	Author	Date
Good to Great: Why Some Companies Make the Leap . . . and Others Don't	Jim Collins	2001
The World is Flat: A Brief History of the Twenty-First Century	Thomas L. Friedman	2005
A Whole New Mind: Why Right-Brainers Will Rule the Future	Daniel H. Pink	2005
Wikinomics: How Mass Collaboration Changes Everything	Don Tapscott	2006
Made to Stick	Chip Heath and Dan Heath	2008
Change by Design	Tim Brown	2009
Delivering Happiness	Tony Hsieh	2010
Business Model Generation: A Handbook For Visionaries, Game Changers, and Challengers	Alex Osterwalder and Yves Pigneur	2010
Steve Jobs	Walter Isaacson	2011
Designing for Growth: A Design Thinking Tool Kit for Managers	Jeanne Liedtka and Tim Ogilvie	2011
Strategy for You	Richard Horwath	2012
Design Works	Heather Fraser	2012
The Idea Factory: Bell Labs and the Great Age of American Innovation	Jon Gertner	2012
Design Thinking for Strategic Innovation: What They Can't Teach You at Business or Design School	Idris Mootee	2013
The Service Innovation Handbook: Action-Oriented Creative Thinking Toolkit for Service Organizations	Lucy Kimbell	2014
Value Proposition Design: How to Create Products and Services Customers Want	Alex Osterwalder, Yves Pigneur, Gregory Bernarda, Alan Smith, and Trish Papadakos	2014
Strategic Design Thinking: Innovation in Products, Services, Experiences and Beyond	Natalie W. Nixon, ed.	2015
Design Thinking: New Product Development Essentials from the PDMA	Michael Luchs and Scott Griffin	2015

Critical Thinking in Management

Peter Drucker—often revered, rarely reviled, but occasionally wrong—was an influential business thinker who considered business as a series of integrated systems of expertise to be collectively managed by individuals with specialized performance focus and skills.[4]

Drucker followed up on Taylor's work around critical thinking to improve performance. But Drucker was by no means the first to ask what it means to think critically. For centuries, observers such as Plato's Socrates had demonstrated that "persons may have power and high position and yet be deeply confused and irrational," further emphasizing the importance of asking questions that seek to establish evidence before we blithely accept ideas as being worthy of belief and action.[5]

At some point, the practice of management shifted from Adam Smith's assertions of the invisible hand in the marketplace to the iron fist of management and self-interest that emerged in an era characterized by a lack of self-restraint or accountability. Still leaders always looked to history for patterns to follow to better understand the importance of information, unpacking assumptions, and going back to basics. Another example of unpacking assumptions was when a revered architect, Ludwig Mies van der Rohe, spurned the label "innovative": "It is better to be good than to be original."[6] It's clear today that expert management requires a more complex reconciliation of these and other diverse values and interests.

The Competitive Context: Differentiation or Atomization

Nobody can escape business school without learning about Porter's Five Forces.[7]

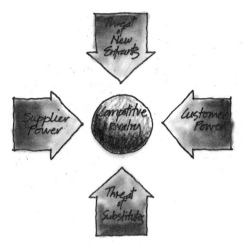

Michael Porter's observations changed the way businesspeople thought about their organization and their business context: It's all about differentiation. Author Gary Hamel says, "It is an unfailing guide to whether some particular strategy, once articulated, can be counted on to produce worthwhile profits."[8] In terms of shifting business thinking, Porter seems to have had in the back of his mind that the building of scenarios and testing ideas against some givens was an important way of approaching business strategy. The operative words, however, were still "competitive" and "profit"; the closing years of the twentieth century had yet to see the lines of systemic failures emerging. The challenge was going to be retaining the engaged energy of competition and the profit motive within a much more complex framework of values and accountability. In the late twentieth century, design and management tried to get better at systematic differentiation; this was about to change with the atomization of information in creative processes.

In a related observation, Thomas Friedman noticed that technology had flattened his perspective to a global level—a change he said that we could greet as an opportunity or as a threat.[9] He urged his readers to think beyond themselves—to their company, their community, and their country—to see the global village or, in a business context, a global marketplace. Friedman uses the visual reference of "flattening" in a powerful way—a key point in the context of designed leadership.

Human Values in Business and Strategic Design

Integrating diverse values in Western business is not new. From the earliest efforts to organize trade and communities under a rule of law (*Magna Carta*, 1215), we have been challenged to reconcile efficiency and fairness in communities and the marketplace. Leading thinkers such as Adam Smith in *The Wealth of Nations* recognized social values and "ingenious arts" in formative governance frameworks.[10] By the mid-twentieth century the importance of human rights to sustainable markets and peaceful cooperation was recognized in the new global order of the United Nations.[11] The latest UN Sustainable Development Goals of 2015 indicate the complexity involved.[12] Whether analyzed as rights, responsibilities, or just prudent risk management, respect for people and strategic design has been a golden thread in the history of good business.

The business academician and theologian Stephen Covey introduced his own observations on character building in *The 7 Habits of Highly Effective People*.[13] Covey's focus on systems of information, of principles and practices, was an early indication to me of the convergence of business and design. Covey's directives could perhaps have benefited from a review of design principles of organization and approach, but the principles reflect similar values: be proactive; begin with an end in mind; put first things first; think win/win; seek first to understand; synergize for combined effects greater than the parts; renew. Perhaps more important, his work and that of others on value theory allowed for the start of a conversation and dialogue among the business and design communities about people and how our habits, places, and products influence our productivity at home and at work.[14]

The Learning Organization

The idea of informed inquiry and learning is nothing new. Joseph Schumpeter was musing on economics on the other side of the Atlantic from Frederick Winslow Taylor when Schumpeter sought to reconcile his observations of the marketplace with a theory of economic development.[15] In the heady days before world wars intervened, he argued that entrepreneurial activity results in "innovation"—which he later characterized as simply new combinations of existing resources or knowledge.[16] Schumpeter recognized that the creation of new technologies and business organizations allowed access to new markets, which started the cycle anew, and that creative destruction could be rationalized and systematized for effectiveness by business teams of trained specialists. When Peter Senge wrote about the Learning Organization, he was looking at the social systems of organizations, and his five disciplines were those of a philosopher looking internally, not of a manager trying to get people working together.[17] His model was perhaps too simple, if only for overlooking millennia of design-based systems thinking, centuries of law, and business systems thinking.

I like that Senge was noting that these skills, also identified as executive functions by cognitive sciences around the same time, are increasingly essential for all workers, not just executives. Others have observed that the ability to learn, unlearn, and relearn is needed not only for sustainable competitive advantage, but also to reconcile powerful, hardwired instincts and biases with the wonders of the digital age. Senge raised the profile of the importance of experimentation and failure—both long-standing and key elements to the strategic-design approach tested by crisis over time.

Leaders and Teams

Jim Collins's classic book *Good to Great* reaffirmed the idea of a level of leadership that blends "personal humility and professional will."[18] The invisible hand was now emerging from the mists of the marketplace with defined attributes. Collins challenged the notion that a great company requires a larger-than-life celebrity leader to take it from good to great, suggesting rather that "leaders channel their ego needs away from themselves and into the larger goal of building a great company."[19]

Strategic Design and Business

The ties of design to business have been developing in the Western world since at least the time of Vitruvius (first century B.C.), at times led by Medici money and at other times led by innovations in the ideas of interest, credit, debt, property, contracts, and organizations themselves, to benefit those less fortunate. From Henry Ford's classic, "If I had asked people what they wanted, they would have said faster horses," to Steve Jobs's extreme attention to detail, from F. W. Taylor's scientific management to the rules of the International Standards Organization, design and business have always been good neighbors. Now, the time has come to learn to talk together better.

The creative industries have been working with design thinking for generations, but the pace of cross-fertilization is picking up. High net worth individuals have always tended to appreciate good design, and low net worth individuals have always benefitted the most from it, but we forget the importance to systems as well as products. As dean of business at the University of Toronto, Roger Martin became an ambassador for design and business with his book, *The Design of Business*.[20] Martin recounts his introduction to design through business cases, in examples from Procter & Gamble and Cirque du Soleil. Moving (with the crowd) away from management-era simplicity, Martin makes the case that we are too reliant on simplistic analytical models and thinking that doesn't move us powerfully enough into what he calls innovation.

Business Model Theory and Innovation

Strategic design is a problem-solving process for application in the marketplace. Therefore, it needs to occur within a framework of other systems. In this regard, Edith Penrose brought an interdisciplinary curiosity and expertise in economics, intellectual property, and global markets to her formative work on the foundations of innovative enterprise.[21] Penrose is also credited with recognizing that people are not simply human resources, but rather members of teams who collectively learn and teach an innovative experience and approach.[22] In my work I realized that getting ideas to work in the marketplace, even under the critical demands of conflict, was not only a task that was carried out by men. In fact, two women are likely the brains behind the information age—not just the creative theory, but the gritty, applied practice of strategic design: 1) Ada Lovelace in the mid-nineteenth century who worked on the Analytic Engine and 2) Lieutenant Commander Grace Hopper[23] in the mid-twentieth century who invented the first compiler for a computer programming language.

Having researched and focused my postgraduate work on systems and a handbook to teach and learn design, I was pleased to find Osterwalder and Pigneur's *Business Model Generation: A Handbook for Visionaries, Game Changers, and Challengers.*[24] This text is an impressive example of the trend to bring together design and business through the creation of the business canvas: a way to make visual the various interactions of the value proposition, the customer, supply chains, financing, revenues, and so on.

This is an exemplary text about the structure and modeling of the business itself in a digital age of accountability and opportunity.

Design Thinking in Business

The most recent wave of works in this field is now also starting to differentiate based on the purposes of the business or management. One such work is Jeanne Liedtka and Tim Ogilvie's *Designing for Growth*.[25] This is a design thinking tool kit for managers, and it provides another good perspective on design thinking in business terms, with useful case examples. The authors offer up their organizing framework for the design process: useful tools for timely responses and a series of questions: *What is?*, *What if?*, *What wows?*, *What works?*. To build on the utility in application, a *Designing for Growth Field Book* followed in 2014.[26] Another example of this type is Lucy Kimbell's *Service Innovation Handbook*, which focuses on user and customer experience.[27] Subtitled *An Action-oriented Creative Thinking Toolkit for Service Organizations* (2014), Kimbell creates a compelling and useful approach to improving the design of innovative services. She brings together various techniques for great service design: ethnography, big data, and prototyping, and provides the reader with an engaging balance of the creative and the critical.

One of the skills of strategic design is to take stock, identify values to filter information, and start to work for elegant solutions that balance diverse interests while making the result look obvious. In an age when more information is added to the public record in a week than Adam Smith had available in his lifetime, the skills and knowledge of strategic design and design thinking will be increasingly essential.

Notes

Introduction

1. SpaceX, *SpaceX Rocket's First Stage Crashes During Landing Attempt*, Space.com video, 1:00, April 15, 2015, http://www.space.com/29119-spacex -reusable-rocket-landing-crash-video.html.

2. Elon Musk, Twitter post, January 15, 2015, 10:56 p.m., https://twitter.com /elonmusk/status/555981841476227072.

3. SpaceX, *SpaceX Sticks a Rocket Landing at Sea in Historic First*, Space.com video, 1:56, April 8, 2015, http://www.space.com/32517-spacex-sticks-rocket -landing-sea-dragon-launch.html.

4. Drake Baer, "Elon Musk on Being a Product-Obsessed 'Nano-Manager': 'It's Not a Recipe for Happiness,'" *Business Insider*, January 12, 2015, http:// www.businessinsider.com/elon-musk-calls-himself-a-nano-manager-2015-1.

5. Angèle is an important colleague as we collaborate in developing our practice of strategic design and experimenting with pedagogical innovations in the d.studio.

6. Angèle Beausoleil, "The Case for Design-Mediated Innovation Pedagogy" (PhD dissertation, University of British Columbia, 2016), 9.

7. "Appreciative Inquiry suggests that human organizing and change, at its best, is a relational process of inquiry, grounded in affirmation and appreciation." See Diana Whitney and Amanda Trosten-Bloom, *The Power of Appreciative Inquiry: A Practical Guide to Positive Change* (San Francisco: Berrett-Koehler, 2003), 1.

8. Ursula Franklin, *The Real World of Technology* (Toronto: Anansi Press, 1990).

9. Moura Quayle, "Urban Countryside—Rural Metropolis" (lecture, The Vancouver Institute, October 25, 1997).

10. J. R. R. Tolkien, *The Lord of the Rings: The Ring Sets Out* (London: Harper-Collins, seven-volume edition, 1999), 224.

11. "Man possesses essentially three brains inside one sole brain structure. The oldest is the 'reptilian brain,' designated 'R-complex,' which consists of the ventral striatum and the basal ganglia. The R-complex [are] the … structures that evolved from the floor of the forebrain during development. '[T]he reptilian brain' was responsible for typical instinctual behaviours, including territoriality, dominance, and aggression." See Marcelo R. Roxo and others, "The Limbic System Conception and Its Historical Evolution," in *The Scientific World Journal* 11, Article 157150 (2011), http://dx.doi .org/10.1100/2011/157150. For the original conception of the reptilian brain, see Paul D. Maclean, *The Triune Brain in Evolution* (New York: Plenum, 1990), 15–18.

12. Angela M. Passarelli, "Opposing Domains Theory" (presentation delivered at Opening Governance: The 75th Annual Meeting of the Academy of Management, August 7–11, 2015, Vancouver, British Columbia).

13. David Fushtey, "Kinds of Organizations for a Global Marketplace," in *The Director and the Manager: Law and Governance in a Digital Age—Machiavelli Had it Easy* (Charlotte, N.C.: InfoAge, forthcoming), chapter 1.

14. Vanessa Timmer and Eleni Sotos, "Accelerating & Amplifying Change: Transforming Consumption & Production Toward Sustainability," *Wingspread October 2013 Workshop Report*, http://scpsystem.weebly.com/oct-2013 -workshop-report.html.

1. Ten Principles for Designed Leadership

1. David Fushtey, *Principled Governance Framework: Briefing Note*, The Governance Counsel, 2003. http://www.governance.dsfw.com/profile.htm.

2. David Fushtey, *The Director and the Manager: Law and Governance in a Digital Age—Machiavelli Had it Easy* (Charlotte, N.C.: InfoAge, forthcoming).

3. David Fushtey is a governance lawyer (the governance guy) in Vancouver, British Columbia. He writes about the emerging discipline of governance, getting along in and out of board rooms, and understanding the importance of the rule of law in everyday life and decisions. http://www.governance.dsfw. com/profile.htm.

4. In urban design you are accountable for financial budgets, timelines, and materials used. You are accountable to your client, regulators (often many); other professionals on the project; the men, women, and children from around the world who will use the project; and to the natural environment of wind and rain and sun—all of which will smite you down if you fail to understand.

5. Horst Rittel, and M. M. Webber, "Wicked Problems," *Man-made Futures* 26, no. 1 (1974): 272–280. Difficult-to-define problems with no specific right answers are often called wicked problems. Coined by Rittel and Webber in this classic planning paper.

6. Gerard Puccio, Mary Murdock, and Marie Mance, *Creative Leadership: Skills That Drive Change* (London: Sage, 2007), 42.

7. Fushtey, "An International Social Finance Zone?", Simon Fraser University Centre for Dialogue (blog), October 9, 2012.

8. David Colcleugh, *Everyone a Leader: A Guide to Leading High-Performance Organizations for Engineers and Scientists* (Toronto: Rotman-UTP, 2013), 69.

9. University of British Columbia, Sauder School of Business d.studio, http://dstudio.ubc.ca. A note of thanks to Denise Withers, cofounder of the d.studio when she was the Learning Designer at Sauder. She now "leads change through story" at http://www.denisewithers.com.

10. University of British Columbia, Sauder School of Business d.studio, "Assumption Dumption," http://dstudio.ubc.ca/toolkit/temporary-techniques/new-6-toolkit-techniques-5-assumption-dumption/. Denise Withers (see note 9) coined the term Assumption Dumption.

11. John Lanchester, "Money Talks: Learning the Language of Finance," *The New Yorker*, August 2, 2014, http://www.newyorker.com/magazine/2014/08/04/money-talks-6.

12. Lanchester, "Money Talks."

13. Hugh Dubberly and others, *Notes on the Role of Leadership & Language in Regenerating Organizations* (2002), http://pangaro.com/littlegreybook.pdf.

14. Louise Chawla, "Reaching Home: Reflections on Environmental Autobiography" (discussion during the Twenty-Fifth Annual Conference of the Environmental Design Research Association, March 16–20, 1994, San Antonio, Texas), reproduced in *Environmental & Architectural Phenomenology Newsletter*, last modified January 16, 2009, http://www.arch.ksu.edu/seamon/Chawla_home.htm.

15. Clare Cooper Marcus, "Environmental Autobiography," *Room One Thousand, Issue 2: Souvenir Nostalgia* (2014), http://two.roomonethousand.com/index/#/environmental-autobiography/.

16. Pamela Druckerman, "Finding Your Place in the World After Graduation," *The New York Times*, May 29, 2015, http://www.nytimes.com/2015/05/31 /opinion/sunday/how-to-find-your-place-in-the-world-after-graduation .html?_r=0.

17. Rachel Kaplan, and Stephen Kaplan, "Bringing Out the Best in People: A Psychological Perspective," *Conservation Biology* 22, no. 4 (2008): 826. See also Rachel Kaplan, "The Role of Nature in the Context of the Work-place," *Landscape and Urban Planning* 26 (1993):193–201; Howard Frumkin, "Beyond Toxicity: Human Health and the Natural Environment," *American Journal of Preventive Medicine* 20 (2001): 234–242; Rachel Kaplan and Stephen Kaplan, "Preference, Restoration, and Meaningful Action in the Context of Nearby Nature," *Urban Place: Reconnecting with the Natural World,* P. F. Bartlett, ed. (Cambridge, Mass.: MIT Press, 2005), 271–298.

18. A. A. Milne, "Solitude," in *Now We Are Six* (New York: Dutton Children's Books, 2009), 11. First published in 1927.

19. Douglas Paterson, "Dualities and Dialectics in the Experience of Landscape," *Design + Values: Council of Educators in Landscape Architecture (CELA) Conference Proceedings, Charlottesville, 1992* (Charlottesville, Virginia: CELA Department of Landscape Architecture, 1992), 148.

20. Paterson, "Dualities and Dialectics," 158–159.

21. Joseph Giacomin, "What is Human-Centred Design?" *The Design Journal: An International Journal for all Aspects of Design* 17, no. 4 (2014): 608.

22. IDEO.org, "Design Kit: The Field Guide to Human-Centred Design," http:// www.ideo.com/work/human-centered-design-toolkit/, recently updated from *Design Kit: The Field Guide* to *Human-Centered Design,* in which they explain their design approach:

> Human-centered design is a creative approach to problem solving and the backbone of our work at IDEO.org. It's a process that starts with the people you're designing for and ends with new solutions that are tailor made to suit their needs. Human-centered design is all about building a deep empathy with the people you're designing for; generating tons of ideas; building a bunch of prototypes; sharing what you've made with the people you're designing for; and eventually putting your innovative new solution out in the world.

23. Susan Cain, "When Collaboration Kills Creativity: The Rise of the New Groupthink and the Power of Working Alone," *Quiet: The Power of Intro-verts in a World that Can't Stop Talking* (New York: Crown, 2012), 71–95.

24. Amanda Cooper, Ben Levin, and Carol Campbell, "The Growing (but Still Limited) Importance of Evidence in Education Policy and Practice," *Journal of Educational Change* 10, no. 2 (2009): 159–171.

25. City of Vancouver, *Greenest City Action Plan*, http://vancouver.ca/green -vancouver/greenest-city-action-plan.aspx.

26. Cooper, Levin, and Campbell, "The Growing (but Still Limited)," 161.

27. Alexandra Lange, "Why Charles Moore (Still) Matters," *Metropolis Magazine*, May 2014, http://www.metropolismag.com/Why-Charles-Moore-Still -Matters/.

28. Kevin Keim, "Introduction," in Charles W. Moore, *You Have to Pay for the Public Life: Selected Essays of Charles W. Moore*, Kevin Keim, ed. (Cambridge, Mass.: MIT Press, 2001), ix–x.

29. The Future of Innovation Summit 2015, Villa Del Grumello, Como, Italy, October 11–13. See http://changelabs.stanford.edu/work/future-innovation -summit.

30. Parsons School of Design is one of the five colleges of The New School located in Greenwich Village, New York City.

31. Charles Moore, Gerald Allen, and Donlyn Lyndon, *The Place of Houses* (New York: Holt, Rinehart and Winston, 1974), 188.

32. Moore, Allen, and Lyndon, *The Place of Houses*, 188.

33. Moore, Allen, and Lyndon, *The Place of Houses*, 188.

34. Moore, Allen, and Lyndon, *The Place of Houses*, 189.

35. Michael Hough, *City Form and Natural Processes* (New York: Van Nostrand Rienhold, 1984), 273.

36. Hough, *City Form and Natural Processes*, 18.

37. Hough, *City Form and Natural Processes*, 20.

38. Hough, *City Form and Natural Processes*, 21.

39. Tim Harford, "Multi-Tasking: How to Survive in the 21st Century," *FT Magazine*, September 3, 2015, http://www.ft.com/cms/s/2/bbf1f84a-51c2 -11e5-8642-453585f2cfcd.html.

40. David Allen, *Getting Things Done: The Art of Stress-Free Productivity* (New York: Penguin, 2003), 138–180.

41. Alex Pentland, *Social Physics: How Social Networks Can Make Us Smarter* (New York: Penguin, 2014).

42. Pentland, *Social Physics*, 209.

43. Pentland, *Social Physics*, 209.

44. Jane Jacobs, *The Death and Life of Great American Cities* (New York: Random House, 1963).

45. Jacobs, *The Death and Life of Great American Cities*, 178.

46. Jacobs, *The Death and Life of Great American Cities*, 152.

47. Jacobs, *The Death and Life of Great American Cities*, 200.

48. Erin Chantry, "Urban Designer Series: Jane Jacobs, The Mother of Urban Design," *At the Helm of the Public Realm* (blog), November 18, 2012, http:// helmofthepublicrealm.com/2012/11/18/urban-designer-series-jane-jacobs/.

49. Christopher Alexander, Sara Ishikawa, and Murray Silverstein, *A Pattern Language* (New York: Oxford University Press, 1977).

50. Alexander, Ishikawa, and Silverstein, *A Pattern Language*, 11.

51. Alexander, Ishikawa, and Silverstein, *A Pattern Language*, 13.

52. Alexander, Ishikawa, and Silverstein, *A Pattern Language*, 59.

53. Alexander, Ishikawa, and Silverstein, *A Pattern Language*, 100.

54. Global Trends, "10 Key Trends to Watch for 2014 (Trends 1 to 5)," November 2013, http://www.globaltrends.com/wp-content/uploads/2013/11/GT_Briefing_November_2013_10_Trends_to_Watch_1_to_5_FINAL.pdf.

55. Carsten Foertsch, "4.5 New Coworking Spaces Per Work Day," *Deskmag*, March 4, 2013, http://www.deskmag.com/en/2500-coworking-spaces-4-5-per-day-741.

56. Alexander, Ishikawa, and Silverstein, *A Pattern Language*, 102.

57. The University of British Columbia Annual Report, *TREK 2000: The Story So Far … 2000–2001.*

2. Strategic Design Method: Ask, Try, Do

1. The Sauder d.studio is the brand for the business studio at the UBC Sauder Business School co-founded by Moura Quayle and Denise Withers in 2009 (http://dstudio.ubc.ca). Denise has since founded her own company at http://www.denisewithers.com. Denise uses story to move people—on purpose.

2. Angèle Beausoleil, "A Visual Translation of Active Learning Inside a Business School Studio: The Case of d.studio at the Sauder School of Business at the University of British Columbia" (working paper, 2015), 1.

3. Introduction to Strategic Design (six five-minute videos written and narrated by Moura Quayle):
Part 1: https://www.youtube.com/watch?v=NSdMMzMX54Y
Part 2: https://www.youtube.com/watch?v=msdm9qbHjts
Part 3: https://www.youtube.com/watch?v=RNMghBIqVRE
Part 4: https://www.youtube.com/watch?v=JTosnodVgBg
Part 5: https://www.youtube.com/watch?v=kBe4zHIP7Pk
Part 6: https://www.youtube.com/watch?v=dV6_xGJL8w4.

4. Peter G. Rowe, *Design Thinking* (Cambridge, Mass.: MIT Press, 1986).

5. John Chris Jones, *Design Methods: Seeds of Human Futures* (New York: Wiley, 1970); Don Koberg and Jim Bagnall, *The Universal Traveler: A Soft-Systems Guide To Creativity, Problem-Solving and the Process of Reaching Goals* (Los Altos, Calif.: Kaufmann, 1974); Moura Quayle and Douglas Paterson,

"Techniques for Encouraging Reflection in Design Education," *Journal of Architectural Education* 42, no. 2 (1989): 28–38.

6. Richard Buchanan, "Wicked Problems in Design Thinking," *Design Issues* 8, no. 2 (1992): 5–21; Stefanie Di Russo, "A Brief History of Design Thinking: The Theory [P2]," *I Think ∴ I Design* (blog), March 31, 2012, http://ithinkidesign.wordpress.com/2012/03/31/a-brief-history-of-design-thinking-the-theory-p2/.

7. Tim Brown, with Barry Katz, *Change By Design: How Design Thinking Transforms Organizations and Inspires Innovation* (New York: Harper Business, 2009); Tim Brown, "Design Thinking," *Harvard Business Review* 86, no. 6 (2008): 84; Tim Brown, "Tales of Creativity and Play," *TED Talks*, May 2008, https://www.ted.com/talks/tim_brown_on_creativity_and_play?language=en; Tim Brown, "Designers—think big!," *TED Talks*, July 2009, https://www.ted.com/talks/tim_brown_urges_designers_to_think_big.

8. E. Manzini and C. Vezzoli, "A Strategic Design Approach to Develop Sustainable Product Service Systems: Examples Taken from the 'Environmentally Friendly Innovation' Italian Prize," *Journal of Cleaner Production* 11, no. 8 (2003): 851–857; Julie H. Hertenstein and Marjorie B. Platt, "Developing a Strategic Design Culture," *Design Management Journal (Former Series)* 8, no. 2 (1997): 10–19.

9. Bryan Boyer, Justin Cook, and Marco Steinberg, *In Studio: Recipes for Systemic Change*; Christian Bason, *Leading Public Sector Innovation: Co-creating for a Better Society* (Bristol: Policy Press, 2010); C. K. Prahalad and Venkat Ramaswamy, "Co-creation Experiences: The Next Practice in Value Creation," *Journal of Interactive Marketing* 18, no. 3 (2004): 5–14.

10. James L. Adams, *The Care and Feeding of Ideas: A Guide to Encouraging Creativity* (Reading, Mass.: Addison-Wesley, 1986), 14, fig. 2-1.

11. Richard Paul, Linda Elder, and Ted Bartell, "Brief History of the Idea of Critical Thinking," http://www.criticalthinking.org/pages/a-brief-history-of-the-idea-of-critical-thinking/408.

12. William Graham Sumner, *Folkways: A Study of the Sociological Importance of Usages, Manners, Customs, Mores, and Morals* (New York: Ginn, 1940), 632.

13. Anthony Kenny, *A Brief History of Western Philosophy* (Oxford: Blackwell, 1998), 35–36; Robert C. Solomon, *The Little Philosophy Book* (Oxford: Oxford University Press, 2008), 4.

14. Paul, Elder, and Bartell, "Brief History of the Idea of Critical Thinking."

15. "The Story of Symbols: The Question Mark," Kuriositas.com, March 21, 2015, http://www.kuriositas.com/2012/05/story-of-symbols.html. See also M. B. Parkes, *Pause and Effect: An Introduction to the History of Punctuation in the West* (Berkeley, Calif.: University of California Press, 1993).

16. Amanda Lang, *Power of Why* (Toronto: HarperCollins, 2012), 11.

17. Yves Behar is the founder and principal designer of Fuseproject, an award-winning industrial design and brand development firm. See http://www.fuseproject.com/.

18. Edwin Heathcote, review of *"Speculative Everything*, by Anthony Dunne and Fiona Raby," *Financial Times*, January 17, 2014, http://www.ft.com/intl/cms/s/2/d9a0f03c-7e9f-11e3-8642-00144feabdco.html.

19. Anthony Dunne and Fiona Raby, *Speculative Everything: Design, Fiction and Social Dreaming* (Cambridge, Mass.: MIT Press, 2013).

20. Dunne and Raby, *Speculative Everything*, 18.

21. Karl Taro Greenfield, "How Mark Parker Keeps Nike in the Lead," *Wall Street Journal Magazine*, November 4, 2015, http://www.wsj.com/articles/how-mark-parker-keeps-nike-in-the-lead-1446689666.

22. David Colander and Roland Kupers, *Complexity and the Art of Public Policy: Solving Society's Problems from the Bottom Up* (Princeton, N.J.: Princeton University Press: 2014), 7.

23. "How might we?" is the very useful question used in *ExperienceInnovation™*—a computer simulation cocreated by IDEO and Experience Point. An explanation of "How Might We" can be found on the IDEO Design Kit site: http://www.designkit.org/methods/3.

24. IDEO and Experience Point, *ExperienceInnovation™*. *ExperienceInnovation* is an educational game created by ExperiencePoint in collaboration with IDEO. *ExperienceInnovation* provides meaningful experience with design thinking; you will collaborate and compete to solve a realistic and complex challenge while engaging with the terms, techniques, and thought patterns of successful innovators.

25. Denise Withers, co-founder of d.studio, has a way with words and coined: Finding Facts, Finding Meaning, Finding Opportunities.

26. Design Council report, "Innovation by Design: How Design Enables Science and Technology Research to Achieve Greater Impact," http://www.designcouncil.org.uk/sites/default/files/asset/document/ innovation-by-design.pdf, 15.

27. Attributed to everyone from Eleanor Roosevelt to Ralph Waldo Emerson and Kurt Vonnegut. The exact match to the quote appeared in Mary Schmich, "Advice, Like Youth, Probably Just Wasted on the Young," *Chicago Tribune*, June 1, 1997, 4C.

28. This phrase, credited to IDEO, helps us to defer judgment and break a massive problem into manageable pieces, http://www.designkit.org/methods/3.

29. Professor Ronald Kellett, director, UBC School of Architecture and Landscape Architecture, is an award-winning architect and researcher. For more information on Ron and his work, see http://www.sala.ubc.ca/people/faculty/ronald-kellett.

30. IDEO and Experience Point, *ExperienceInnovation™*.

31. Design Council, "Innovation by Design," 15.

32. Ted Levitt, "Creativity Is Not Enough," *Harvard Business Review*, (2002), 72.

33. Markus Baer, "Putting Creativity to Work: The Implementation of Creative Ideas in Organizations," *Academy of Management Journal* 55, no. 5 (2012): 1102.

34. Baer, "Putting Creativity to Work," 1116.

35. Michael A. West, "Ideas Are Ten a Penny: It's Team Implementation Not Idea Generation That Counts," *Applied Psychology* 51, no. 3 (2002): 411–424.

36. Björn Malbert, "Participatory Approaches to Sustainable Urban Development: Reflections on Practice in Seattle, Vancouver and Waiketere," *Planning Practice & Research* 13, no. 2 (1998): 183–189.

3. Thinking Visually and Spatially

1. World Economic Forum Annual Meeting 2010, Davos-Klosters, Switzerland, January 27–31, https://www.weforum.org/agenda/2009/09/improve-the-state-of-the-world-rethink-redesign-rebuild/.

2. New York Times Conference: The Next New World: Work 2.0, UCSF Mission Bay Conference Center, San Francisco, June 12, 2014.

3. Andrew McAfee, remarks made at the *New York Times* Next New World Conference, June 12, 2014, UCSF Mission Bay Conference Center, San Francisco. For more on McAfee and the MIT Initiative on Digital Economy, see http://mitsloan.mit.edu/ide/. For McAfee on technology as complement, see "Mastering the Three Worlds of Information Technology," *Harvard Business Review*, November 2006, https://hbr.org/2006/11/mastering-the-three-worlds-of-information-technology?cm_sp=Topics-_-Links-_-Read%20These%20First.

4. Eileen Dombrowski, Lena Rotenberg, and Mimi Bick, *Theory of Knowledge for IB Diploma Programme* (Oxford: Oxford University Press, 2013), vi–vii.

5. Dombrowski, *Theory of Knowledge for IB Diploma Programme*, vi–vii.

6. Ronald Heifetz, Alexander Grashow, and Marty Linsky, "Leadership in a (Permanent) Crisis," *Harvard Business Review*, July-August, 2009, https://hbr.org/2009/07/leadership-in-a-permanent-crisis.

7. Heifetz, Grashow, and Linsky, "Leadership in a (Permanent) Crisis."

8. Cram101 Textbook Reviews, *Just the Facts101: Textbook Key Facts for Money, the Financial System, and the Economy by R. Glenn Hubbard*, 6th ed (ebook study guide), "Chapter 16, Banking in the International Economy."

9. Thomas Friedman, "How to Get a Job at Google," *The New York Times*, February 22, 2014, http://www.nytimes.com/2014/02/23/opinion/sunday/friedman-how-to-get-a-job-at-google.html?_r=0.

10. James Manyika and others, "Disruptive Technologies: Advances That Will Transform Life, Business, and the Global Economy," McKinsey Global Institute report, May 2013, http://www.mckinsey.com/insights/business_technology/disruptive_technologies.

11. Colin Ware, *Visual Thinking for Design* (Burlington, Mass.: Kaufmann, 2008), ix.

12. Ware, *Visual Thinking for Design*, 165.

13. On the discovery and first use of glass, see Seth C. Rasmussen, *How Glass Changed the World: The History and Chemistry of Glass from Antiquity to the 13th Century* (New York: Springer Heidelberg, 2012), 11; for mention of glass in Aristophanes, see Aristophanes, *Clouds* 731–775, William James Hickie, trans., *The Comedies of Aristophanes* (London: Henry G. Bohn, 1853), 731–775; on the first telescope, see Patrick Moore, *Eyes on the Universe: The Story of the Telescope* (London: Springer-Verlag, 1997), 6–12.

14. Rolf Willach, "The Long Route to the Invention of the Telescope," *Transactions of the American Philosophical Society* New Series 98, no. 5 (2008): 1–3.

15. Frank N. Egerton, "A History of the Ecological Sciences, Part 19: Leeuwenhoek's Microscopic Natural History," *Bulletin of the Ecological Society of America* 87, no. 1 (January 2006): 47–48.

16. David Brewster, *The Kaleidoscope: Its History, Theory, and Construction*, second edition (London: Murray, 1858), 1.

17. Shane Speck, "How 3-D PC Glasses Work," in HowStuffWorks.com, December 12, 2003, http://www.howstuffworks.com/3d-pc-glasses4.htm.

18. Clayton Christensen, Jeff Dyer, and Hal Gregersen, *The Innovator's DNA: Mastering the Five Skills of Disruptive Innovators* (Boston: Harvard Business School Publishing, 2011), 1.

19. Price Waterhouse Coopers, *Good to Grow: 2014 US CEO Survey*, U.S. report, 17th Annual Global CEO Survey, http://www.pwc.com/us/en/ceo-survey-us/2014/assets/2014-us-ceo-survey.pdf.

20. Christenson, Dyer, and Gregersen, *The Innovator's DNA*, 23–25.

21. Norman Crowe and Paul Laseau, *Visual Notes for Architects and Designers* (New York: Van Nostrand Reinhold, 1984), 6.

22. Ware, *Visual Thinking for Design*, 148–149.

23. Ware, *Visual Thinking for Design*, 164.

24. Centre for Spatial Studies, University of Redlands, http://spatialstudies.redlands.edu.

25. "University of Redlands Faculty Projects," University of Redlands Centre for Spacial Studies, http://univredlands.maps.arcgis.com/apps/MapJournal/index.html?appid=1b1634e20fb8465ca39c35a3253ae452&webmap=6024bd7b011e46d68b2764782d3495e1.

26. Moura Quayle, "Urban Countryside—Rural Metropolis" (lecture, The Vancouver Institute, October 25, 1997).

27. Douglas Paterson, "Visual/Verbal Transformation" (lecture notes, University of British Columbia, November 1989). Special thanks to Professor Paterson, who explored these transformations in depth and taught his students to understand them and use them in his theory classes and his studios.

28. Crowe and Laseau, *Visual Notes for Architects and Designers*, 1.

29. Jonah Lehrer, *Imagine: How Creativity Works* (New York: Houghton Mifflin, 2012).

30. Emphasis added. See Lehrer, *Imagine: How Creativity Works*, 69.

31. Global Trends, *GT Briefing December 2014: 10 Trends to Watch for 2015*, http://www.globaltrends.com/?s=Global+Trends+Briefing+december+2014%3A+10+Trends+to+Watch+for+2015.

4. Places to Practice Designed Leadership

1. The Eberly Center for Teaching Excellence and Educational Innovation at Carnegie Mellon University, "Labs / Studios," Carnegie Mellon University, https://www.cmu.edu/teaching/designteach/design/instructionalstrategies/labsstudios.html.

2. Daved Barry and Stefan Meisiek, "Discovering the Business Studio," *Journal of Management Education* 39, no. 1 (2015): 156.

3. Barry and Meisiek, "Discovering the Business Studio," 158.

4. "MIT Media Lab," Massachusetts Institute of Technology, School of Architecture + Planning, http://www.media.mit.edu/about/about-the-lab; Bryan Boyer, Justin W. Cook, and Marco Steinberg, *In Studio: Recipes for Systemic Change* (Helsinki: Sitra, 2011); "Strategic Innovation Lab (sLab)," OCAD University (formerly the Ontario College of Art and Design), http://slab.ocadu.ca/about; Institute Without Boundaries, George Brown College, http://institutewithoutboundaries.ca/about-us/overview/. http://institutewithoutboundaries.ca/about-us/overview/; Social Innovation Lab, Waterloo Institute for Social Innovation and Resilience, https://uwaterloo.ca/waterloo-institute-for-social-innovation-and-resilience/; Department of Design & Innovation, Weatherhead School of Management, Case Western Reserve University, https://weatherhead.case.edu/departments/design-and-innovation/; Hasso

Plattner Institute of Design at D.School at Stanford University, https://dschool.stanford.edu; and HPI School of Design Thinking, Potsdam, Germany, http://hpi.de/en/school-of-design-thinking/hpi-d-school/background.html.

5. Christian Bason, *Leading Public Sector Innovation: Co-creating for a Better Society* (Bristol, UK: Policy Press, 2010); Lucy Kimbell, *Applying Design Approaches to Policy Making: Discovering Policy Lab* (Brighton, UK: University of Brighton, 2015).

6. The d.studio is the business studio in the UBC Sauder School of Business. The Policy Studio is located in the UBC Liu Institute for Global Issues.

7. Commerce 388—Design Methods for Business Innovation: Studio Practice—at UBC has grown from twenty students meeting once a year to thirty-six students meeting three times per year. The current population of the studio is twenty-four Bachelor of Commerce students and twelve students from across the university: arts, science, engineering, and environmental design. This collaborative and interdisciplinary environment is great preparation for the student who wants to be more "work ready" as each studio works closely with business clients.

8. The Copenhagen Business School hosted a Studio Summit in August 2014, where close to thirty participants shared ideas and best practices around studios, mainly those hosted in business schools.

9. Barry and Meisiek, "Discovering the Business Studio," 166.

10. Barry and Meisiek, "Discovering the Business Studio," 167.

11. Saras D. Sarasvathy, "Causation and Effectuation: Toward a Theoretical Shift from Economic Inevitability to Entrepreneurial Contingency," *Academy of Management Review* 26, no. 2 (2001): 243–263.

12. Barry and Meisiek, "Discovering the Business Studio," 167.

13. Roberto Verganti, in conversation with author at Politecnico di Milano, June 4, 2010. Roberto is the author of *Design-Driven Innovation: Changing the Rules of Competition by Radically Innovating What Things Mean* (Boston: Harvard Business Press, 2009).

14. Daniel Fallman, "The Pragmatics of Design Studio Culture: Our Story" (workshop paper presented at the CHI Conference on Human Factors in Computing Systems 2007, San Jose, Calif., April 28–May 3, 2007); Clark Kellogg, "The Studio Culture Summit: An Overview Report for the 2004 Studio Culture Summit, October 8–10, 2004, University of Minnesota" (Seattle, Wash.: American Institute of Architecture Students, 2005).

15. David Fleming, "Design Talk: Constructing the Object in Studio Conversations," in *Design Issues* 124, no. 2 (1998): 41–62.

16. Gabriela Goldschmidt and William L. Porter, eds., *Design Representation* (London: Springer-Verlag, 2004).

17. Stefani Ledewitz, "Models of Design in Studio Teaching," *Journal of Architectural Education* 138, no. 2 (1985): 2–8; Moura Quayle and Douglas Paterson, "Techniques for Encouraging Reflection in Design Education," *Journal of Architectural Education* 42, no. 2 (1989): 28–38.

18. Jennifer D. Webb and Nancy G. Miller, "Some Preparation Required: The Journey to Successful Studio Collaboration," *Journal of Interior Design* 31, no. 2 (2006): 1–9.

19. Angèle Beausoleil, "Strategic Design and a Business School Studio: The Case of d.studio at the Sauder School of Business at the University of British Columbia," (draft conference paper, Studio Summit at the AoMO Creativity + Design conference, Copenhagen, August 28–31, 2014), 4.

20. Beausoleil, "Strategic Design and a Business School Studio," 8.

21. Mary Lou Maher, Simeon J. Simoff, and Anna Cicognani, *Understanding Virtual Design Studios* (London: Springer-Verlag, 2012).

22. Angela Carbone, and Judy Sheard, "A Studio-Based Teaching and Learning Model in IT: What Do First Year Students Think?" in ITiCSE '02: Proceedings of the 7th Annual Conference on Innovation and Technology in Computer Science Education, Aarhus, Denmark, June 24–26, 2002 (New York: ACM, 2002), 213–217.

23. "Columbia Design Challenge: Confronting the Ebola Crisis," Columbia University, Columbia Engineering, The Fu Foundation School of Engineering and Applied Science, http://engineering.columbia.edu/columbia-design-challenge-confronting-ebola-crisis.

24. Angèle Beausoleil, Marcelo Bravo, and Steve Williams, "UBC Design Challenge Participant Workbook," University of British Columbia, http://blogs.ubc.ca/designchallenge/files/2015/10/UBC_DChallenge_Workbook_lowres.pdf.

5. Learning and Education for Designed Leadership

1. Aristotle, *The Nicomachean Ethics* 2.1, W. D. Ross, trans., (Raleigh, N.C.: Generic FL Freebook Publisher [ebook], 2000), 13. Also available from The Internet Classics Archive, http://classics.mit.edu/Aristotle/nicomachaen.2.ii.html.

2. Email correspondence with Steve Alisharan, professor of accounting at the UBC Sauder School of Business, November 21, 2015. Net present value (NPV) is a metric that is used to determine the profitability of a project that will span more than one year. It is the net result of subtracting the present value of all of the cash outflows at different points in time from the present value of all of the cash inflows that are received at different points in time. The term "present value" refers to the time value of money concept. Because

money has a time value (a dollar received today is not the same as a dollar received one year from now), we should not compare cash flows that are received or paid out at different points in time. By bringing all cash flows to their present value we are minimizing the impact of comparing cash flows that are received or paid out at different points in time.

3. Donald A. Schön, *The Reflective Practitioner: How Professionals Think in Action* (London: Ashgate, 1983).

4. Schön, *The Reflective Practitioner*, 68.

5. Mark K. Smith, "Donald Schön: Learning, Reflection and Change," *The Encyclopedia of Informal Education*, July 2001, http://infed.org/mobi/donald -schon-learning-reflection-change/.

6. Talula Cartwright, "Feeling Your Way: Enhancing Leadership Through Intuition," *Leadership in Action* 24, no. 2 (May/June 2004), 24.

7. Though originally rendered in Greek as "σπεῦδε βραδέως," the Latin translation "festina lente" was later used by several leaders throughout the Middle Ages and Renaissance. For Augustus's use of the motto, see C. Suetonius Tranquillus, *De Vita Caesarum, Divus Augustus* 25.4, Robert Graves, ed. and trans., in *The Twelve Caesars* (London: Penguin, 1979), 62.

8. Moura Quayle, and Douglas Paterson, "Techniques for Encouraging Reflection in Design," *Journal of Architectural Education* 42, no. 2, 30.

9. Carol S. Dweck, *Mindset: The New Psychology of Success* (New York: Ballantine, 2008), 215.

10. Herminia Ibarra, *Act Like a Leader, Think Like a Leader* (Watertown, Mass.: Harvard Business Publishing, 2015), 5.

11. David Boud, Rosemary Keogh, and David Walker, eds., *Reflection: Turning Experience into Learning* (Oxford: RoutledgeFalmer, 1985).

12. Anne Hungerford, instructor, Advanced Study in Writing for Business and the Professions, Simon Fraser University, 1985.

13. Moura Quayle, "Using Writing Techniques in the Design Studio," in CELA 89: Proceedings from the Council of Educators in Landscape Architecture Annual Conference, September 7–9, 1989, Amelia Island Plantation, Amelia Island, Florida (Washington, DC: Landscape Architecture Foundation, 1990), 65–68.

14. Henriette Anne Klauser, *Writing on Both Sides of the Brain: Breakthrough Techniques for People Who Write* (San Francisco: Harper and Row, 1986), 69–87.

15. Walker, "Writing and Reflection," *Reflection: Turning Experience into Learning*, 53.

16. Bruce Lloyd, "Leadership and Learning," *Leadership & Organization Development Journal* 15, no. 4 (1994): 19.

17. Angèle Beausoleil, and Moura Quayle, Workbook, UBC Design Challenge, October 2–4, 2015, Vancouver Campus, http://dstudio.sites.olt.ubc.ca /files/2016/12/UBC_DChallenge_FinalReport.pdf.

18. Management Mentors, http://www.management-mentors.com/resources /coaching-and-mentoring.

19. Insala.com, "How Does Mentoring Help Leaders and Managers Grow and Develop?" http://www.insala.com/Articles/leadership-coaching/how-does -mentoring-help-leaders-and-managers-grow-and-develop.asp.

20. Jim Horwath, "Leadership and Mentoring of Young Employees," in SANS Technology Institute, Leadership Lab: Management Competencies, http:// www.sans.edu/research/management-laboratory/article/horwath-421-leader.

21. Roderick Ian Eddington, "Team Captain," *Monocle Magazine* 8, no. 74 (June 2014): 88.

22. Richard Barker, "No, Management Is Not a Profession," *Harvard Business Review* (July-August 2010): 52–60.

23. S. K. Clinebell, and J. M. Clinebell, "The Tension in Business Education Between Academic Rigor and Real-World Relevance: The Role of Executive Professors," *Academy of Management Learning & Education* 7, no. 1 (2008): 99–107.

24. Clinebell and Clinebell, "The Tension in Business Education," 99–107.

25. Eric Cornuel, "Challenges Facing Business Schools in the Future," *The Journal of Management Development* 26, no. 1 (2007): 87–92.

26. Anne Colby and others, *Rethinking Undergraduate Business Education: Liberal Learning for the Profession* (San Francisco: Jossey-Bass, 2011).

27. Austin Carr, "The Most Important Leadership Quality for CEOs? Creativity," *Fast Company*, May 18, 2010, http://www.fastcompany.com/1648943/most -important-leadership-quality-ceos-creativity.

28. Harvard Business School: The HBS Difference, http://www.hbs.edu/mba/the -hbs-difference/Pages/default.aspx.

29. "Why Fuqua," Duke University, The Fuqua School of Business, http://www .fuqua.duke.edu/daytime-mba/why-fuqua/.

30. Anonymous editor, preface to Abraham Zaleznik, "Managers and Leaders: Are They Different?" *Harvard Business Review*, January 2004, https://hbr .org/2004/01/managers-and-leaders-are-they-different.

31. Susie Burroughs, Kay Brocato, and Dana Franz, "Problem Based and Studio Based Learning: Approaches to Promoting Reform Thinking Among Teacher Candidates," *National Forum of Teacher Education Journal* 19, no. 3 (2009): 1–15.

32. Inci Basa, "Project Selection in Design Studio: Absence of Learning Environments," *The Educational Forum* 74, no. 3 (2010): 213–226.

33. Donald Schön, *The Design Studio: An Exploration of Its Traditions and Potentials* (London: RIBA Publications for RIBA Building Industry Trust, 1985).

34. THNK School of Creative Leadership, http://www.thnk.org/.

35. Design Council, "The Value of Design: Factfinder Report" (2007), https://www.designcouncil.org.uk/sites/default/files/asset/document/TheValueOf DesignFactfinder_Design_Council.pdf.

36. The Design ROI Project was a research project conducted between September 2011 and September 2012 with the aim of developing a model and a set of metrics for measuring the return on investments in design. The project was funded by Aalto University, the Finnish Funding Agency for Technology and Innovation (Tekes) and fifteen member agencies of the Finnish Design Business Association (FDBA). "DROI—Measurable Design" is a summary of the information gathered, the main findings and the solutions developed during the research project. See Heidi Cheng, Kristian Keinänen, and Maria Salo, "DROI—Measurable Design," Design ROI Project Report (Helsinki: Arts Promotion Centre Finland, 2012), http://www.seeplatform.eu/images /DROI%20Measurable%20Design(1).pdf.

6. Designed Leadership Cases

1. David Pendleton, "Personality and Leadership Matrix," International Executive Development Programs (IEDP.com blog), January 11, 2011, http://www .iedp.com/articles/personality-and-leadership-matrix/.

2. Jean Woodall, "MBAs Are Focusing on a New World Order," interview in *Director Magazine*, March 10, 2011.

3. Miki Kashton, "Want Teamwork? Encourage Free Speech," *The New York Times*, April 12, 2014, http://www.nytimes.com/2014/04/13/jobs/want-teamwork -encourage-free-speech.html.

4. Gregor Robertson and others, *Greenest City: Quick Start Recommendations*, report to Vancouver City Council, April 27, 2009, http://vancouver.ca/files /cov/greenestcity-quickstart.pdf.

5. City of Vancouver, *Greenest City Action Plan*, http://vancouver.ca/green -vancouver/greenest-city-action-plan.aspx.

6. Robertson and others, *Vancouver 2020: A Bright Green Future,* report to Vancouver City Council (October 2009), http://vancouver.ca/files/cov/bright -green-future.pdf.

7. Postsecondary institutional members of C3: British Columbia Institute of Technology, Emily Carr University of Art and Design, Langara College,

Simon Fraser University, the University of British Columbia, and Vancouver Community College. See Vancouver mayor's office press release, "Campus-City Collaborative (C3) Connects the City with Post-secondary Institutions to Advance Job Creation Goals," December 8, 2011, http://www.mayorofvancouver.ca/campus%25e2%2580%2590city-collaborative-c3-connects-the-city-with-post%25e2%2580%2590secondary-institutions-to-advance-job-creation-goals.

8. Simon Fraser University Centre for Dialogue, "Carbon Talks: Solutions for a Low-Carbon Economy," See website for Carbon Talks, www.carbontalks.ca.

9. Carbon Talks, SFU Centre for Dialogue, *Vancouver as a Global Urban Sustainability Centre: Dialogue Report* (June 13, 2012), PDF available at http://www.carbontalks.ca/resources/reports/?page=2.

10. CityStudio, http://citystudiovancouver.com. Kudos to Janet Moore and Duane Elverum who co-founded CityStudio and remain committed to the concept of "the city is the classroom."

11. Joaquin Rodriguez Alvarez, Alistair Cole, Joerg Knieling, and Moura Quayle, "Leading Cities: Lessons from Building a Transdisciplinary Global Urban Policy Network" (unpublished paper, 2015).

12. World Class Cities Partnership, *Talent Magnets: Cities and Universities Building the Workforce for a Knowledge Economy*, https://leadingcities2014.files.wordpress.com/2014/02/talent-report-final-draft.pdf; Leading Cities, *Co-Creating Cities: Defining Co-Creation as a Means of Citizen Engagement*, https://leadingcities2014.files.wordpress.com/2014/02/co-creation-formatted-draft-6.pdf; Leading Cities, *Co-Creation Connectivity: Addressing the Citizen Engagement Challenge*, https://leadingcities2014.files.wordpress.com/2015/09/co-creation-connectivity.pdf.

13. Richard Florida is the author of *The Rise of the Creative Class, And How It's Transforming Work, Leisure and Everyday Life* (New York: Basic Books, 2002). For more, see http://www.creativeclass.com/richard_florida.

14. World Class Cities Partnership, *Talent Magnets*, 1.

15. Pacific Coast Collaborative, http://pacificcoastcollaborative.org

16 West Coast Infrastructure Exchange, http://westcoastx.com/.

17. Bruce Katz, and Owen Washburn, "Innovations to Watch," *The Brookings Institution*, January 18, 2013, http://www.brookings.edu/research/interactives/2013/innovationstowatch#Governance.

18. The commitments include: account for cost of carbon pollution in each jurisdiction; affirm the need to inform policy with findings from climate science; enlist the support of research on ocean acidification and take action to combat it; continue deployment of high-speed rail across the region; support emerging markets and innovation for alternative fuels in commercial trucks, buses, rail, ports, and marine transportation; transform the market for energy

efficiency and lead the way to "net-zero" buildings; and make infrastructure climate-smart and investment ready. For more information, see http://www .pacificcoastcollaborative.org/.

19. *Pacific Coast Climate Leadership Action Plan* http://www.pacificcoastcollab-orative.org/Documents/PCC_Leadership_Action_Plan_060116_signed.pdf.

20. I want to thank Bryant Fairley and Paul Irwin of the BC government. With-out their hard work and leadership, the Pacific Coast Collaborative would never have sustained itself.

21. Urban Landscape Task Force, *Greenways-Public Ways*, report to Vancouver City Council (May 1992). See also Moura Quayle, "From Urban Greenways and Public Ways: Realizing Public Ideas in a Fragmented World," *Landscape and Urban Planning* 33, no. 3 (1995): 461–475.

22. Moura Quayle, "Opinion: B.C. Needs to Take Green Economy to the Next Level," *The Vancouver Sun*, April 26, 2011.

7. Take-Away

1. Urban Landscape Task Force, *Greenways-Public Ways*, report to Vancouver City Council (Vancouver, May 1992), 80.

Appendix: The Evolution of Strategic Design in Business Thinking

1. Daniel Muzyka, in personal communication with the author, Spring 2009. Muzyka is the current CEO of the Conference Board of Canada. As dean at Sauder for thirteen years, he invited entrepreneurial activities, including design, into Sauder and shaped the school as it is today.

2. Frederick Winslow Taylor, *The Principles of Scientific Management* (New York: Harper, 1911). For Henry Ford on production systems and observa-tions on organizational behavior, see Henry Ford, *My Life and Work* (New York: Garden City, 1922); and *My Philosophy of Industry* (London: Harrap, 1929). Dale Carnegie, *How to Win Friends and Influence People* (New York: Simon and Schuster, 1936).

3. Taylor, *The Principles of Scientific Management*, 5.

4. Peter F. Drucker, *The Practice of Management: A Study of the Most Impor-tant Function in American Society* (New York: Harper, 1954).

5. Richard Paul, Linda Elder, and Ted Bartell, "A Brief History of the Idea of Critical Thinking," *California Teacher Preparation for Instruction in Critical Thinking: Research Findings and Policy Recommendations: State of California, California Commission on Teacher Credentialing, Sacramento California, 1997* (Sacramento: Foundation for Critical Thinking, 1997), http://www.criticalthinking.org/pages/a-brief-history-of-the-idea-of-critical-thinking/408.

6. Ludwig Mies van der Rohe, as quoted in Gideon Fink Shapiro, "Is It Better to Be Good Than Original?" *The Svbtxt Journal*, February 10, 2014, https://svbscription.com/blog/is-it-better-to-be-good-than-original.

7. Michael E. Porter, "The Five Competitive Forces That Shape Strategy," *Harvard Business Review*, January 2008, 86–104.

8. Gary Hamel, as quoted in *Business: The Ultimate Resource* (Cambridge, Mass.: Perseus, 2002), 901.

9. Thomas Friedman, *The World is Flat: A Brief History of the Twenty-First Century* (New York: Farrar, Straus and Giroux, 2005).

10. Adam Smith, *An Inquiry into the Nature and Causes of the Wealth of Nations* (New York: Knopf, 1910, 1991).

11. United Nations General Assembly, *The Universal Declaration of Human Rights*, ratified December 16, 1948, www.un.org/en/universal-declaration-human-rights.

12. United Nations General Assembly, *Transforming Our World: The 2030 Agenda for Sustainable Development*, resolution adopted on September 25, 2015, https://sustainabledevelopment.un.org/post2015/transformingourworld.

13. Stephen Covey, *The 7 Habits of Highly Effective People* (New York: Free Press, 1989).

14. Daniel Kahneman, *Thinking, Fast and Slow* (Toronto: Doubleday Canada, 2011); Stephen Gilliland, Dick Steiner, and Daniel Skarlicki, eds., *Emerging Perspectives on Values in Organizations* (Greenwich: Information Age, 2004).

15. Joseph Schumpeter, *Theorie der wirtschaftlichen Entwicklung* (Leipzig: Verlag von Duncker & Humblot, 1911), Opie Redvers, trans., in Joseph Schumpeter, *The Theory of Economic Development: An Inquiry into Profits, Capital, Credit, Interest, and the Business Cycle* (New Brunswick, NJ: Transaction Books, 1983).

16. William Lazonick, "Business History and Economic Development," *The Oxford Handbook of Business History*, Geoffrey Jones and Jonathan Zeitlin, eds. (Oxford: Oxford University Press, 2007), 67–95.

17. Peter Senge, *The Fifth Discipline: The Art and Practice of the Learning Organization* (New York: Currency Doubleday, 1990).

18. Jim Collins, *Good to Great: Why Some Companies Make the Leap . . . And Others Don't* (New York: HarperCollins, 2001), 21.

19. Collins, *Good to Great*, 10, 21.

20. Roger L. Martin, *The Design of Business: Why Design Thinking Is the Next Competitive Advantage* (Boston: Harvard Business, 2009).

21. Edith Penrose, *The Theory and Growth of the Firm* (New York: Wiley, 1959).

22. Lazonick, "Business History and Economic Development," 70–71 on the contributions of Edith Penrose.

23. Kurt Beyer, *Grace Hopper and the Invention of the Information Age* (Cambridge, Mass.: MIT Press, 2009).

24. Moura Quayle, *Ideabook for Teaching Design* (Mesa, Ariz.: PDA, 1985). Alexander Osterwalder and Yves Pigneur, *Business Model Generation: A Handbook for Visionaries, Game Changers, and Challengers* (Hoboken, NJ: Wiley, 2010).

25. Jeanne Liedtka, and Tim Ogilvie, *Designing for Growth: A Design Thinking Tool Kit for Managers* (New York: Columbia Business School, 2011).

26. Jeanne Liedtka, Tim Ogilvie, and Rachel Brozenske, *The Designing for Growth Field Book: A Step-by-Step Project Guide* (New York: Columbia Business School, 2014).

27. Lucy Kimbell, *The Service Innovation Handbook: Action-oriented Creative Thinking Toolkit for Service Organizations* (Amsterdam: BIS, 2014).

Works Cited

Adams, James L. *The Care and Feeding of Ideas: A Guide to Encouraging Creativity*. Reading, Mass.: Addison-Wesley, 1986.

Alexander, Christopher, Sara Ishikawa, and Murray Silverstein. *A Pattern Language: Towns, Buildings, Construction*. Oxford: Oxford University Press, 1977.

Bason, Christian. *Leading Public Sector Innovation: Co-creating for a Better Society*. Bristol, UK: Policy Press, 2010.

Boyer, Bryan, Justin W. Cook, and Marco Steinberg. *In Studio: Recipes for Systemic Change*. Helsinki: Sitra, 2011.

Brown, Tim, with Barry Katz. *Change by Design: How Design Thinking Transforms Organizations and Inspires Innovation*. New York: Harper Business, 2009.

Cain, Susan. *Quiet: The Power of Introverts in a World That Can't Stop Talking*. New York: Crown, 2012.

Colander, David, and Roland Kupers. *Complexity and the Art of Public Policy: Solving Society's Problems from the Bottom Up*. Princeton, N.J.: Princeton University Press, 2014.

Colcleugh, David. *Everyone a Leader: A Guide to Leading High-Performance Organizations for Engineers and Scientists*. Toronto: Rotman-UTP, 2013.

Collins, Jim. *Good to Great: Why Some Companies Make the Leap ... and Others Don't*. New York: HarperCollins, 2001.

Covey, Stephen. *The 7 Habits of Highly Effective People: Powerful Lessons in Personal Change*. New York: Free Press, 1989.

Crowe, Norman, and Paul Laseau. *Visual Notes for Architects and Designers*. New York: Van Nostrand Reinhold, 1984.

De Bono, Edward. *Six Thinking Hats*. London: Penguin, 2000.

Dombrowski, Eileen, Lena Rotenberg, and Mimi Bick. *Theory of Knowledge for IB Diploma Programme.* Oxford: Oxford University Press, 2013.

Drucker, Peter F. *The Practice of Management.* New York: Harper, 1954.

Fraser, Heather. *Design Works: How to Tackle Your Toughest Innovation Challenges Through Business Design.* Toronto: Rotman-UTP, 2012.

Friedman, Thomas L. *The World Is Flat: A Brief History of the Twenty-First Century.* New York: Farrar, Straus and Giroux, 2005.

Fushtey, David. *The Director and the Manager: Law and Governance in a Digital Age—Machiavelli Had It Easy.* Charlotte, N.C.: InfoAge, forthcoming.

Heath, Chip, and Dan Heath. *Made to Stick: Why Some Ideas Survive and Others Die.* New York: Random House, 2008.

Hough, Michael. *City Form and Natural Processes.* New York: Van Nostrand Reinhold, 1984.

Ibarra, Herminia. *Act Like a Leader, Think Like a Leader.* Watertown, Mass.: Harvard Business Publishing, 2015.

Isaacson, Walter. *Steve Jobs.* New York: Simon & Shuster, 2011.

Isaacson, Walter. *The Innovators: How a Group of Hackers, Geniuses, and Geeks Created the Digital Revolution.* New York: Simon & Schuster, 2014.

Jacobs, Jane. *The Death and Life of Great American Cities.* New York: Random House, 1963.

Kaplan, Rachel, and Stephen Kaplan. *Urban Place: Reconnecting with the Natural World.* Edited by P. F. Bartlett. Cambridge, Mass.: MIT Press, 2005.

Kimbell, Lucy. *The Service Innovation Handbook: Action-oriented Creative Thinking Toolkit for Service Organizations.* Amsterdam: BIS, 2014.

Klauser, Henriette Anne. *Writing on Both Sides of the Brain: Breakthrough Techniques for People Who Write.* San Francisco: Harper and Row, 1986.

Koberg, Don, and Jim Bagnall. *The Universal Traveler: A Soft-Systems Guide To: Creativity, Problem-Solving and the Process of Reaching Goals.* Los Altos, Calif.: Kaufmann, 1974.

Liedtka, Jeanne, and Tim Ogilvie. *Designing for Growth: A Design Thinking Tool Kit for Managers.* New York: Columbia Business School, 2011.

Luchs, Michael, and Scott Griffin. *Design Thinking: New Product Development Essentials from the PDMA.* Hoboken, New Jersey: Wiley-Blackwell, 2015.

Martin, Roger L. *The Design of Business: Why Design Thinking Is the Next Competitive Advantage.* Boston: Harvard Business, 2009.

Moore, Charles, Gerald Allen, and Donlyn Lyndon. *The Place of Houses.* New York: Holt, Rinehart and Winston, 1974.

Mootee, Idris. *Design Thinking for Strategic Innovation: What They Can't Teach You at Business or Design School.* Hoboken, N.J.: Wiley, 2013.

Nixon, Natalie W., ed. *Strategic Design Thinking: Innovation in Products, Services, Experiences and Beyond.* New York: Bloomsbury, 2015.

Osterwalder, Alex, Yves Pigneur, Gregory Bernarda, Alan Smityh, and Trish Papdakos. *Value Proposition Design: How to Create Products and Services Customers Want.* Hoboken, N.J.: Wiley, 2014.

Osterwalder, Alexander, and Yves Pigneur. *Business Model Generation: A Handbook for Visionaries, Game Changers, and Challengers.* Hoboken, N.J.: Wiley, 2010.

Pink, Daniel H. *A Whole New Mind: Why Right-Brainers Will Rule the Future.* New York: Riverhead Books, 2005.

Porter, Michael E. *Competitive Strategy: Techniques for Analyzing Industries and Competitors.* New York: Free Press, 1980.

Puccio, Gerard, Mary Murdock, and Marie Mance. *Creative Leadership: Skills That Drive Change.* London: Sage, 2007.

Quayle, Moura. *Ideabook for Teaching Design.* Mesa, Ariz: PDA, 1985.

Schön, Donald A. *The Reflective Practitioner: How Professionals Think in Action.* London: Ashgate, 1983.

Senge, Peter. *The Fifth Discipline: The Art and Practice of the Learning Organization.* New York: Doubleday, 1990.

Ware, Colin. *Visual Thinking for Design.* Burlington, Mass.: Kaufmann, 2008.

Wesley, Frances, and Cheryl Rose, Katharine McGowan, Kirsten Robinson, Ola Tjornbo, and Mark Tovey. Social Innovation Lab Guide, 2016. https://uwaterloo .ca/waterloo-institute-for-social-innovation-and-resilience/sites/ca.waterloo -institute-for-social-innovation-and-resilience/files/uploads/files/10_silabguide _final.pdf.

Whitney, Diana, and Amanda Trosten-Bloom. *The Power of Appreciative Inquiry: A Practical Guide to Positive Change.* San Francisco: Berrett-Koehler, 2003.

Index